Will I See My Dog *in* Heaven?

Will I See My Dog *in* Heaven?

God's Saving Love for the Whole Family of Creation

Jack Wintz, OFM

PARACLETE PRESS
BREWSTER, MASSACHUSETTS

Will I See My Dog in Heaven?

2009 First Printing

Copyright © 2009 by Jack Wintz

ISBN 978-1-55725-568-6

Unless otherwise noted all scriptural references are taken from the *New American Bible with Revised New Testament and Revised Psalms* © 1991, 1986, 1970 Confraternity of Christian Doctrine, Washington, D.C., and are used by permission. All Rights Reserved. No part of the *New American Bible* may be reproduced in any form without permission in writing from the copyright owner.

Scriptural references marked NAB 1986 in this work are taken from the *New American Bible with Revised New Testament* © 1986, 1970 Confraternity of Christian Doctrine, Washington, D.C. and are used by permission of the copyright owner. All Rights Reserved. No part of the *New American Bible* may be reproduced in any form without permission in writing from the copyright owner.

Scriptural references marked JB are taken from *The Jerusalem Bible* © 1966 by Darton Longman & Todd Ltd and Doubleday and Company Ltd. Used by permission. All rights reserved.

Scriptural references marked NRSV are taken from the *New Revised Standard Version of the Bible,* copyright 1989, 1995 by the Division of Christian Education of the National Council of Churches of Christ in the United States of America and are used by permission. All rights reserved.

Library of Congress Cataloging-in-Publication Data

Wintz, Jack.
  Will I see my dog in heaven? : God's saving love for the whole family of creation / Jack Wintz.
    p. cm.
  Includes bibliographical references (p.   ).
  ISBN 978-1-55725-568-6
  1. Animals—Religious aspects—Christianity. 2. Future life—Christianity. 3. Animals—Religious aspects—Catholic Church. 4. Future life—Catholic Church. I. Title.
  BT746.W56 2009
  231.7--dc22   2009000259

10 9 8 7 6 5 4 3 2 1

Published by Paraclete Press
Brewster, Massachusetts
www.paracletepress.com

Printed in the United States of America using paper with 30% post-consumer waste. Trees were responsibly harvested following sustainable forestry guidelines. No trees from ancient forests were used in the making of the paper.

for my confrere and longtime friend MURRAY BODO, OFM

Contents

Introduction

How do we answer children when they ask, "Will I see my dog in heaven?" Such a question can become one of the most important in our lives, striking to the heart of a child's faith in both life and God. But "Will I see my dog in heaven?" is, as I see it, an urgent concern for adults as well. We adults have an equally deep desire to know if we will see our pets again, and all the other lovely creatures alongside whom we now inhabit this planet. What will become of them after they die?

A friend of mine, Anne, told me the following story:

Anne lives in Cincinnati, where a few years ago she faced the important questions of death and eternity for an animal companion as she was present at the death of her dearly loved dog, Miss Daisy. Anne had befriended Miss Daisy some ten years earlier when the dog, of mixed Spaniel origin, was barely one year old. With the help of her adult son, Anne rescued Miss Daisy from Cincinnati's inner city.

"I would see Miss Daisy wandering around the neighborhood where I worked at an elementary school," Anne told me. "I came to realize that the dog was obviously a stray and lost—and she was adorable! I took cans of tuna to the area where Miss Daisy hung out, but she was very afraid of people and wouldn't approach the tuna till she was left alone. My rescue attempts went on for many months."

In time, Anne was successful in winning Miss Daisy's confidence and was able to take her to her home on the outskirts of the city.

"Miss Daisy was still very shy," Anne told me, "but she eventually became a loyal and loving member of our family. Realizing that Miss Daisy needed a companion, I went to the dog pound and came home with a dog named Andy. For ten years or so Miss Daisy and Andy were very happy companions, and both became cherished members of the family. But I became especially attached to Miss Daisy.

"Eventually, Miss Daisy became ill, and we had to make the very difficult decision to have her 'put down.' My son and I took Miss Daisy to the veterinarian so he could put her to sleep. We wanted the vet to come out to our car so Miss Daisy would be in familiar surroundings and we could be holding her, but he refused our request. So we had to take Miss Daisy inside. We laid the gravely ill dog on the vet's table on her special blanket. We petted Miss Daisy gently and spoke softly to her as the vet got everything ready to give her the injection. Miss Daisy lay there quietly for a few seconds, and then, just before the injection took effect, she lifted her head and looked directly into my eyes. I can still see that look. It was as if she knew what was going on and she was saying good-bye."

Anne recalls how her heart melted, and to this day tears come to her eyes when she remembers that scene.

"I still miss the loving pet who had been my dear friend for so many years. *I know I will see Miss Daisy again!*"

I'm sure that most of us have your own memories of being profoundly grief-stricken at the death of a beloved pet. These are not childish concerns, but the mature reflections of loving Christians.

Many of us prefer to pose the question "Will I see my dog in heaven?" in broader spiritual or theological terms. There is more involved in this question than simply wondering if we will ever be reunited with a loved animal companion. For instance, does God's plan of salvation include only humans, or does it include animals, too? In even broader terms, does God intend the *whole* created world to be saved?

As a Franciscan friar for over fifty years, I am very familiar with the stories of St. Francis of Assisi and his close relationship with animals, and these stories have informed the way that I view these things. Perhaps you've heard the stories of this brown-robed friar preaching to the birds, releasing Brother Rabbit from a trap, or letting Sister Raven serve as his "alarm clock" to awaken him for early morning prayer. I've known for a long time that historians have credited St. Francis with composing one of the first great poems in the Italian language—a poem, or hymn, usually entitled *The Canticle of the Creatures*. In this hymn, sometimes known as *The Canticle of Brother Sun,* St. Francis invites all his brother and sister creatures to praise their Creator—Brother Sun and Sister Moon, Brother Fire and Sister Water, as well as Sister Earth, our mother, with all her various fruits and vividly colored flowers.

But for years I have pondered the question *Why did St. Francis do all of this?* Deep down, what intuition inspired St. Francis to call them "brother" and "sister"? Some thirty years ago I came to the conclusion, which I've never abandoned, that Francis came to see that *all creatures form one family of creation.* Maybe that conclusion is obvious to some or most of you. But for me this idea dawned quite gradually—after many years of getting better acquainted with the life and teachings of the saint. Once Francis's understanding dawned on me, the conviction has only grown stronger and stronger. This book has grown out of this conviction, and explores the implications of it. What would it mean if all creatures were one family? How would it affect us? How would it change our understanding about God, and about how we relate to God and to each other?

The central purpose of this book, therefore, is to seriously explore the title question, "Will I see my dog in heaven?" But from the start, I am exploring this question in the context of this broader question, "Does God intend the whole created world to share in God's saving plan?" In the chapters that follow, I present a good bit of evidence—from the Bible and from Christian tradition—and make a rather strong suggestion of what I believe God desires. I introduce St. Francis of Assisi early into this discussion because he has played such a powerful role in shaping my life, and in enhancing all of humanity's love and respect for the created world. He was one of the most amazing and unique personalities of the thirteenth century, and he has continued to appeal to people of almost every religious persuasion for the last 800 years. For example, Matthew Arnold, the nineteenth-century British poet, referred to Francis as "a figure of most magical power and charm." I believe that the teachings and life of Francis can lead us to discover God's will and saving plan for the whole family of creation.

For more than thirty-six years, I have worked as a writer and editor for *St. Anthony Messenger*, a national Catholic magazine, published by the Franciscan friars of Cincinnati. In our July 2003 issue, we printed an article that I wrote, entitled: "Will I See My Little Doggy in Heaven?" The article generated a lively reaction from our readers, and we received a larger than usual number of letters, suggesting that the topic of animals in heaven is truly a *live* issue. I am happy to share with you a few of these letters, published two months later in our September 2003 issue.

• • • • •

[Dear editors:] Happy days are here again for this 69-year-old who happens to be a lifelong lover of cats! After reading Father Jack Wintz's article "Will I See My Little Doggy in Heaven," I feel for the first time real hope for all those cats I've lost to incurable illness and old age over the years, and for the countless numbers of abused, abandoned, and suffering animals the world over. That article made my day!
[From Doris in Hyattsville, MD]

[Dear editors:] I was thoroughly shocked that the editors of a supposed Catholic magazine would publish "Will I See My Little Doggy in Heaven?"

I was taught that only human beings had immortal souls and free will and, therefore, were able to earn either heaven or hell. When did that change?

How do dogs and other animals know what is right or wrong? Will pit bull dogs trained to kill go to hell for doing what they were trained to do? To quote St. Francis because of his love of nature is a totally unfair interpretation of his ideas.
[From Clayton in Santa Clarita, CA]

The opinions of good Christians are clearly divided on this matter.

We know little for certain about the kind of life we are destined to spend with God in the future, or how animals and other creatures will be included in the picture. But clues abound in three vast available sources—Scripture, our Judeo-Christian tradition, and the example of St. Francis—and all of these sources strongly suggest that other creatures besides humans are included in God's plan of salvation. In the ten chapters of this book you will find much evidence and many hints that God desires the whole family of creation, both humans and animals, to be redeemed and saved. But let's begin with the beginning.

Will I See My Dog *in* Heaven?

And It Was Very Good

1.

In the earliest verses of Genesis, darkness covered everything until God created light to separate the darkness from the light. "And God saw that the light was good" (Genesis 1:4, NRSV). Soon we read that God separated the earth from the seas. "And God saw that it was good" (Genesis 1:10). Then God added vegetation, plants, trees, and fruit. "And God saw that it was good" (1:12). On the fourth day, God put two great lights in the sky: the greater light to rule the day and the lesser light to rule the night, thus separating light from darkness. "And God saw that it was good" (1:18). These two great lights, which St. Francis would call "Brother Sun" and "Sister Moon," have contributed enormously to the well-being and enjoyment of God's creatures.

On the fifth day, God created sea monsters and birds of all kinds. "And God saw that it was good" (1:21). On the sixth day, God made land creatures of every kind: "cattle and creeping things and wild animals of the earth of every kind. And God saw that it was good" (1:25). Also on the sixth day, God made human beings, saying, "Let us make humankind in our image, according to our likeness; and let them have dominion over the fish of the sea, and over the birds of the air, and over the cattle, and over all the wild animals of the earth" (1:26).

Finally, in Genesis 1:31, "God saw everything that he had made, and indeed, it was very good." This "very good" label, which God places here upon both human and nonhuman creatures, seems to me to be an argument for God's desire to have *both* classes of creatures share in the original Garden of Paradise, where peace and harmony reigned between God and human beings, upon creature and creature. Certainly, God is not going to create—and then ignore—what he perceives as "very good" creatures.

Would not the Creator's very decision to create the universe and all the creatures that dwell within it imply an unwritten covenant, or agreement, between God and these creatures? This becomes all the more apparent as we discover throughout the Old and New Testaments that "God is Love, and those who abide in love abide in God and God abides in them" (1 John 4:16). This and other passages help us see that God does *everything* out of love, and this includes the creation of our world. God's words to the people of Israel in Jeremiah 31:13 (NRSV) also come to mind: "I have loved you with an everlasting love." The Psalms, too, often remind us that God's "steadfast love endures forever." In Psalm 136 (NRSV) alone, the refrain "his steadfast love endures forever" is repeated some twenty-five times. We can also cite the celebrated passage in John's Gospel: "For God so loved the world that he gave his only Son, so that everyone who believes in him may not perish but may have eternal life" (John 3:16).

But before we get ahead of ourselves, let's look more closely at the Genesis story to discover what we know of God simply as a Creator.

Our God is a God of overflowing love, goodness, and beauty who is ready to give over everything to those he loves. This goodness is reflected in the whole family of creation. When God says of any creature, whether human or nonhuman, that it is "good" or "very good," it is not simply a matter of moral goodness. The creature also has an inherent goodness and beauty—a beauty that reflects God, who is Beauty itself. Surely the Creator would not suddenly stop loving and caring for the creatures he had put into existence with so much care.

In the original picture we have of the Garden of Eden before the fall, Adam and Eve and all the creatures are living together happily in peace and harmony in the presence of a loving God—a wonderful and insightful glimpse of the paradise that is to come.

It makes sense to me, therefore, that the same loving Creator who arranged for these animals and other nonhuman creatures to enjoy happiness in the original Garden would not want to exclude them from the *final* paradise. If they were happy and enjoying God's presence, according to their abilities, in that first Garden, would not God also want them to be happy and enjoy the same in the restored garden?

Father Don Miller, a Franciscan colleague of mine, also lives in Cincinnati. He recently told me a sad story from his childhood. Don's dog Boots, a young German Shepherd, was tragically killed by a car he had been chasing.

"I was devastated," recalls Don, who was nine years old at the time. "On the verge of tears, I asked my parents: 'Is Boots in heaven and will I see him there some day?'

"This little episode happened in Peoria, Illinois, and my parents took me downtown to Sacred Heart Church to talk with Father Baldwin Schulte, the Franciscan pastor there. I asked Fr. Baldwin whether I would see Boots in heaven. He thought for a moment, and then he turned to me and said: 'Yes, you will see your dog in heaven—if that is what it takes to make you happy.'"

Don reflects, "Now as I look back as an adult, I believe Fr. Baldwin's answer was very wise. Instead of giving me a lot of theology, he basically said that in heaven God will see to it that all who live there are supremely happy. Pastorally, it was a very sound and sensitive answer for me at that time. Once we pass on to the next life and see God face to face, as the glorious source of all that exists, those kinds of questions may not seem so important."

Just as the original Creation was very good with animals as a part of it, so too, it seems, our future lives will be very good and will include animals. No one should presume to tell you or me that we will never again see our pets that died many years ago.

I recall learning in my theology classes that in God there is no past, present, or future. There is only an "eternal now." Who can say, therefore, that the God who created all things does not hold in memory all the creatures God has ever made? They were created as good, all of creation was very good together, and there's no reason why that should change in the eternal future.

The Internet, I believe, can actually give us some insights into the ways that God exists and has his being in infinite reach and power. Just as I can instantly communicate electronically with a friend on the other side of the globe or Google all sorts of information at the click of a key, our infinite and loving God can "Google" in a blink the divine memory bank and access any creature he wants. We all exist in God's eternal now. The World Wide Web is an apt symbol of the infinite reach of God and of God's power to bring a whole universe together into one big loving family of creation.

The creation story in Genesis says nothing about the future, only about those initial moments when all things were made. But we wonder what will happen in the afterlife—in the new heaven and the new earth that is to come (Revelation 21:1)? This is a big-time mystery. There are many things about our future paradise that surpass human understanding. We simply do not know what awaits us in heaven. As St. Paul tells the Corinthians, "We teach what scripture calls *the things that no eye has seen and no ear has heard, things beyond the mind of man, all that God has prepared for those who love him*" (1 Corinthians 2:9, JB, emphasis added).

And yet, as Paul told the Athenians at the Areopagus, God is also incredibly near: "He is not far from any one of us. For 'in him we live and move and have our being'; as even some of your own poets have said" (Acts 17:27–28). All creatures experience God in ways that may always remain mysterious.

The Garden of Eden is not only a story or parable of the way the world was created; it is also a metaphor for the final paradise that our loving Creator envisioned before time began. The prophet Isaiah amplifies this theme when he proclaims that after the Messiah's mission is complete, "the wolf shall be a guest of the lamb, and the leopard shall lie down with the kid; the calf and the young lion shall browse together, with a little child to guide them" (11:6). Biblical commentator John F. A. Sawyer describes this passage from Isaiah as a "view of paradise regained." Similarly, a footnote in the Jerusalem Bible says it represents the "peace of Eden" being restored.[1]

This vision of Isaiah—and that of other inspired biblical writers—provides good evidence that the harmony all creatures enjoyed with God and with each other in the beginning of the creation account is really God's picture of what will prevail at the end of our story. When God in the beginning looked upon all creatures and declared that they were "very good," God was not making a useless or careless claim. He meant something enduring was happening—had been set into motion.

Humanity's attempt to play God, however, destroyed the original harmony that humankind had enjoyed with God in the Garden. And we inherited this propensity to sin and the resulting separation from our first parents. We continue to struggle to achieve harmony with other human beings and the created world. Humanity's rejection of God's first blessings had profound results: banishment from the garden, grinding human toil, enmity, and violence with one's neighbors. The prophets proclaimed that war and oppression would fall upon various peoples because of their sins. They also foretold the coming of a Messiah from the line of King David. And they foretold a time to come when all creation would again be very good—indeed, even better than very good. When the mission of the Messiah is completed, those who walk in step with God's love will enjoy an era of forgiveness, reconciliation, justice, and peace.

We have already enjoyed the vision of peace and reconciliation presented above by the prophet Isaiah (11:6).
We now look at a similar peaceful scene painted by the
prophet Amos:

> The days are coming now
> —it is Yahweh who speaks—
> when harvest will follow directly after plowing,
> the treading of grapes soon after sowing,
> when the mountains will run with new wine
> and the hills all flow with it.
> I mean to restore the fortunes of my people Israel;
> they will rebuild the ruined cities and live in them,
> plant vineyards and drink their wine,
> dig gardens and eat their produce.
> (Amos 9:13–14, JB)

What about "Dominion"?

After God made the first man and woman, he told them to "have dominion over the fish of the sea and over the birds of the air and over every living creature that moves upon the earth" (Genesis 1:28, NRSV). In order to put this instruction from God into a proper context, we should take a closer look at just what kind of "dominion" God handed over to human beings.

The first thing we see is that the human style of dominion is meant to imitate very closely God's style as Creator of the world. When we investigate God's way of exercising dominion over the world and its creatures, whether nonhuman or human, we see a Creator who is loving, gentle, thoughtful, and wise. God creates in a reverent and caring way, making sure that everything is "good" at every stage. God "blesses" the first man and woman and exhorts them to "be fruitful and multiply" (Genesis 1:28). Like a proud parent, God watches as the earth brings forth vegetation, seed-bearing plants, and living things of every kind. God provides a beautiful garden watered by lovely rivers. There is never a sense that God is acting in a domineering or exploitative way. God's dominion is one of respect, not of heavy-handed domination. *This* is the way that humans are meant to exercise dominion over their sister and brother creatures and the created world.

Keith Warner, OFM, is a lecturer and a researcher at Santa Clara University in California. He authored *Care for Creation: A Franciscan Spirituality of the Earth* together with Ilia Delio, OSF, and Pamela Wood. In the following brief excerpts from that book, Warner comments on the meaning of *dominion* in the context of a Franciscan spirituality for our times:

> The word *dominion* has a very different connotation today in our scientific industrial society, than in the ancient Near East. God's dominion over all of creation, and our human dominion over the Earth is to echo the love, care, and responsibility that God has toward the created world. God's dominion is founded upon love and justice; it could not be exploitative or abusive.

"Francis's practice of humility," says Warner, colored Francis's approach to creatures. "Francis was a brother to all creation. . . . Francis rejected power, ownership, and authority for himself. He wanted to be humble, to live in solidarity with creation just as Christ did through the Incarnation."

And then:

> Learning how to live in relationship is funda-
> mental. . . . Francis was open to relationship,
> to receiving from all, whether leper, human
> brother, or sister, worms, birds, bishops,
> water, fire, wind, or Blessed Mother Earth.
> Francis recognized the Incarnate Word of God
> in all living creatures. His openness meant he
> could recognize the blessing of being brother
> to all, and his response was humility. He did
> not practice domination or authority but
> sought to live as a cocreature.[2]

For Whom Is This Future Intended?

It is difficult for those who take the Incarnation seriously,
and who adhere to a profound creation spirituality, to
imagine a final paradise without the creatures that God
first created, as well. In Isaiah's case, we see the presence
of peace-blessed animals (such as the wolf lying down
with the lamb), while in the vision of Amos we see an
earthly mix of godly gifts (mountains, hills, vineyards,
and flowing wine).

When I try to visualize the final paradise in which animals and humans live together in peace and harmony, I often think of animal blessings that I have taken part in. This is particularly true on the Feast Day of St. Francis, when churches all over the world hold "Blessing of the Animals" services, in which the creatures are often invited into the sanctuary and offered special blessings as members of God's family. An ideal alternative setting for such a ceremony is a park or a church courtyard with lots of trees and flowers in it and perhaps a fountain or a pool of water.

Ironically, when people bring their pets from different parts of town, there can be disharmony and trouble. Dogs start barking at cats and people struggle to keep animals from fighting, growling, and hissing. But often in my experience, once the blessings begin, a spirit of harmony and peace prevails among pets and people.

(In later chapters, you will read about animal blessings I have attended that resemble the peaceable kingdom described in the Bible.)

Many Christians believe that nonhuman creatures do not have a place in heaven. The reasoning seems to go like this: life with God after death is only possible for human beings who have received the gift of new life with God through baptism. Only humans have intelligence and free will and thus have the capacity to enjoy fullness of life in heaven. Similarly, animals and other nonhuman creatures do not have human souls and are thus excluded from heaven, according to this mindset.

My comment is this: when we consider the story of Adam and Eve before their disobedience, and we look at the animals, the birds, the fish, the trees and plants in the Garden of Eden, they all seem to be in harmonious and happy relationship with God and with Adam and Eve.

True, the nonhuman creatures do not have human souls, but they obviously have some kind of principle of life in order to do the things they do. An animal that shows affection and loyalty, for example, surely has some kind of "soul" or inner light that allows it to enjoy life and give great joy to its caretakers. A bird that sings a beautiful melody contributes to the world of art and, by reflecting the beauty of its Maker, gives us a bit of heaven in the process. There are a lot of things we just don't know about life with God, and one of these things is how nonhumans participate in that life.

One thing we *do* know from the Genesis stories is that animals, plants, and other creatures found happiness in the first Paradise. Why then would God—or anyone else—want to exclude them from the paradise that is yet to come? Just as we find clues in the Book of Genesis that God wants animals and other nonhuman creatures to share such joys, so we will also, in the chapters ahead, find clues in other books of Scripture, and elsewhere, that reveal this same desire on the part of God.

I refer again to the article I wrote for *St. Anthony Messenger* magazine back in 2003—the one that prompted me to write this book. Well, here is another letter that we received in response:

[Dear editors:] I am still jumping up and down over the article about animals in heaven. All observations made by Father Jack are sound references to the fact that God loves all creation and will include all in our heavenly home.

For the past several years, I have organized a "Blessing of the Animals." In 1972, I had written to Mother Teresa [of Calcutta] to ask for a letter of support. She sent one, over her own signature, and I quote: "[Animals] too are created by the same hand of God which created us. As we humans are gifted with intelligence, which the animals lack, it is our duty to protect them and to promote their well-being. We also owe it to them as they serve us with such docility and loyalty."

I think Mother Teresa says all there is to say about the sacredness of the animal kingdom.

[From Marlene, Louisville, KY]

Marlene's comment about the "sacredness of the animal kingdom" is only a short step away from the central theme of *Will I See My Dog in Heaven?*—the sacredness of the whole family of creation.

2.

Noah and Jonah

Both of these popular biblical stories —the first from the book of Genesis, the second from the book of Jonah—reveal God's desire to save not only the people of the earth but the animals as well.

Noah and the Ark

The story of Noah and the ark is simple—it couldn't be more familiar, could it? Most of us knew it as very young children. But our understanding grows, just as our bodies do.

For me, the ark is a wonderful symbol of God's desire to save the whole family of creation. This story makes it very apparent that God's plan is not to save humankind apart from other creatures. We are all in the same boat, so to speak, humans and other creatures alike. As St. Paul writes to the Romans (8:22), "All creation is groaning" for its liberation.

To get the flavor of this ancient story, we turn to Genesis 6:5–8:[3]

> The Lord saw that the wickedness of human-kind was great in the earth, and that every inclination of the thoughts of their hearts was only evil continually. And the Lord was sorry that he had made humankind on the earth, and it grieved him to his heart. So the Lord said, "I will blot out from the earth the human beings I have created—people together with animals and creeping things

and birds of the air, for I am sorry that I have made them." But Noah found favor in the sight of the Lord.

Because of the widespread wickedness at that time, God tells Noah that he is going to destroy everything living on the earth as well as the earth itself. God instructs Noah to build a huge ark with a roof, three decks, a door on the side, and many other specifications.

I am amazed at God's care and solicitude for *all* the creatures in the ark, and this applies to the animals also, not just to Noah and the other humans. God shows his love and care in bringing aboard the ark "every kind" of creature (wanting no species to go extinct) and that they should be "male and female" alike (insuring the continuation and propagation of each of these species). God doesn't want Noah to pack them in the back of a big truck and rush them off to some safe place. No, God wants Noah to be more caring about the details, as well as about all these brother and sister creatures. For example, Noah is to take with him "every kind of food" and to "store it up; and it shall serve for food for you and for them. Noah . . . did all that God commanded" (see Genesis 6:19–21).

"Then the Lord said to Noah, 'Go into the ark, you and all your household, for I have seen that you alone are righteous before me in this generation'" (Genesis 7:1). When we stop to see what's really happening in this story, we find that Noah's righteousness truly imitates the righteousness of God. For God's care focuses not only upon the human family but also upon the whole family of creation as well. We see that the animals and other creatures are now part of Noah's "household" and in his care, just as they had been under God's loving care from the beginning. To imitate the broad solicitude of our Creator, a good human leader must care not only for other human beings, but also for the earth and for the wider family of creation.

"And Noah with his sons [Shem, Ham, and Japheth] and his wife and his sons' wives went into the ark to escape the waters of the flood (7:7). . . . And after seven days the waters of the flood came on the earth" (7:10).

Even as children who have heard the story well know, it rained for forty days and forty nights. We also recall that after the rain stopped, Noah opened the window of the ark and sent out a dove to see if the waters had subsided, but since the dove had no place to land, it returned to Noah in the ark. Noah waited seven days, and sent the dove out again. This time the dove came back in the evening with an olive leaf. This assured Noah that the waters were subsiding. After waiting another seven days, he sent out the dove, and this time the dove did not return, indicating that the flood was over. Noah and his wife and their three sons and their wives—and all the animals—had survived. All were perfectly safe in the ark.

Let's pause for moment and take a closer look at that dove. The episode of Noah and the dove is a little story within the bigger story, and it reinforces the idea that God's plan is not to save the humans apart from the other creatures. In fact, the "little story" itself suggests that humans and other creatures are actually meant to help one another reach our common salvation. What might it mean, if we came to understand humans and animals as helping each other on the way to union with God?

We can find many other instances in the Bible (and in our own lives) in which God's other creatures collaborate with us in our journey toward salvation and in carrying out God's designs. Consider, for example, the donkey in the Gospel account that carried Christ during his triumphal entry into Jerusalem (see Luke 19:29–38). Or think of an occasion in your own life—when you see a beautiful flower on a spring day, for example, and it lifts your heart to praise your Creator. Or consider how often in the book of Psalms the psalmist, upon seeing the sun and moon and shining stars and other beautiful creatures, is inspired to invite these creatures to join the human family in singing God's praises, thus drawing us all closer to our Creator and our God-given destiny (see Psalm 148).

But let's get back to the bigger story of Noah. That story is not yet finished, even though the flood has gone away. After the waters subsided and dried up, Noah's household along with all the other creatures left the ark. "Then Noah built an altar to the Lord, and took of every clean animal and of every clean bird, and offered burnt offerings on the altar. And when the Lord smelled the pleasing odor, the Lord said in his heart, 'I will never again curse the ground because of humankind . . . nor will I ever again destroy every living creature as I have done'" (Genesis 8:20–21).

At this point, "God blessed Noah and his sons, and said to them, 'Be fruitful and multiply, and fill the earth'" (Genesis 9:1). Interestingly, this is exactly what God told the first man and woman immediately after God created them "in his image" in Genesis 1:28. Apparently, God is telling Noah and his sons (and their wives, obviously), that this is a "new creation" and a "second chance." This time God backs up his pledge, to never again destroy human beings and other living creatures, with a solemn covenant. It's important to note that the covenant is made not only with Noah and his descendants but also *with the other living creatures*, the animals and birds that had been on the ark (see Genesis 9:8–10). This seems to suggest that those other creatures communicate with God, in their own ways, in ways that may be similar and equivalent to our own communications with him.

In God's own words, "I establish my covenant with you, that never again shall all flesh be cut off by the waters of a flood, and never again shall there be a flood to destroy the earth" (Genesis 9:11). As if to show how serious this pledge is, God introduces a dramatic sign— the rainbow. "God said, 'This is the sign of the covenant that I make between me and you and every living creature that is with you, for all future generations: I have set my bow in the clouds, and it shall be sign between me and the earth'" (Genesis 9:12–13).

Thus in the story of Noah and the ark, there is no way to mistake that God's plan is to save the human family along with the rest of creation. And God backs this plan up with a covenant—which specifically includes "every living creature"—never again to destroy the whole family of creation. God punctuates this pledge with the rainbow, a sign of hope, arching across the whole family of creation.

Jonah and the Whale:
A Parable of God's Inclusive Love

Just as most of us heard the story of Noah as children, the book of Jonah also reads like a children's story: there is a furious storm at sea. The sailors throw Jonah into the raging water when they discover that Jonah caused the storm. The seas calm. There is a lesson to be learned, or "taken away" from the story and into our lives.

Jonah had tried to run far away from the task God had asked of him: to preach to the city of Nineveh, the capital city of the Assyrians. Now, the Assyrians were the longtime enemies of the Israelites. It is no surprise then that the Israelites, Jonah among them, felt very little love for the Ninevites. Jonah was not at all pleased that God's saving love included the likes of them. (You may find it interesting to know that the ruins of ancient Nineveh can still be seen today across the Tigris River opposite Mosul in northern Iraq.)

God, however, arranged for a big fish to swallow Jonah. Jonah, in turn, repented of his disobedience. He was in the belly of the fish "three days and three nights" (Jonah 1:17). He pleaded for the Lord to deliver him. He offered thanks and pledged obedience to the Lord, saying, "What I have vowed I will pay. Deliverance belongs to the Lord!

Then the Lord spoke to the fish, and it spewed Jonah out upon the dry land" (2:9b–10).

The story of Jonah is really a parable of God's all-embracing love. It is amazing to realize that once again *even the animals are included in God's saving plan.* You may not have noticed this part of the story. When Jonah proclaimed to the people of Nineveh, "Forty days more and Nineveh will be overthrown," the people and the king of Nineveh were very responsive. "[The king] rose from his throne, removed his robe, covered himself with sackcloth [rough clothing], and sat in ashes" (3:6). Then the king made a decree: "No human being or animal, no herd or flock, shall taste anything. They shall not feed, nor shall they drink water. Human beings and animals shall be covered in sackcloth, and they shall cry mightily to God. All shall turn from their evil ways and from the violence that is in their hands" (3:7–8).

When God saw that the people *and* the animals turned from their evil ways, God changed his mind about the calamity that was to befall the city and withheld all punishment. Jonah became very angry because God's mercy and forgiveness extended beyond the chosen people and included their enemies, the people of Nineveh. Jonah confessed that it was precisely the idea of God's merciful and inclusive love that drove him to flee away from God's request that he preach to the people of Nineveh in the first place. Now, no doubt, it made Jonah angrier still to know that God wanted to save *even the animals* in this story.

Jonah then went outside the city and made a hut for himself. He sat there waiting to see what would happen to the city. God, meanwhile, provided a bush for Jonah to help shade his head and bring a bit of comfort. For this Jonah was very happy and grateful. But the next day God had a worm attack the bush, causing it to wither. When the sun rose and beat down on Jonah's head, Jonah asked that he might die, saying, "It is better for me to die than to live" (4:8b).

God asked Jonah whether it is right for him "to be angry about the bush." Jonah replied, "Yes, angry enough to die" (4:9). To this the Lord replied, "You are concerned about the bush, for which you did not labor and which you did not grow; it came into being in a night and perished in a night. And should I not be concerned about Nineveh, that great city, in which there are more than a hundred and twenty thousand persons who do not know their right hand from their left, and also many animals?" (4:10–11).

This intriguing question ends the story: God's point seems to be that, if Jonah can throw a big snit about a little bush for which Jonah did not even lift his little finger, why should not the loving Creator of the universe be concerned about the great city of Nineveh and all the human beings and animals that live there?

Just as in the story of Noah and the ark, when a dove was used by Noah to assist in God's plan to save the whole family of creation, so now in this amazing, inspired story of Jonah, we see a big fish taking a similar role. The fish plays a key function in helping the reluctant Jonah carry out God's plan to save the people of Nineveh. Again, this seems to be an example of an animal or a creature helping us on our way to salvation. We are a part of the Creation, not *apart from* it. We should also note that— even in the saving of Nineveh—the animals of Nineveh are given an important role in performing the penances that help win God's mercy for the city.

God uses a bush and a worm to lead the narrow-minded Jonah to a better understanding of the inclusive nature of God's saving love. Human beings and other creatures are meant to help each other in our common journey toward our future life with God.

Animals in our own day can teach us a lot about rising above our narrow-mindedness and intolerance. We see dogs, cats, and other pets showing great affection to their owners, whether these owners be rich or poor, black or white, beautiful or disfigured, healthy or sick. I have a clear memory of a volunteer coming regularly to a nursing home a few years ago with a young Collie dog to visit my mother and other residents of that home. That dog certainly gave great comfort to my mom, who was coping with cancer at the time. The dog, with the full approval of the volunteer, had no qualms whatsoever about lying alongside my ninety-four-year-old mother as she lay propped up in bed. She was so happy to pet and enjoy this wonderful creature on her final journey toward life with God.

The stories of Noah and Jonah have much to teach us about God's inclusive love, and about *our* role in collaborating respectfully with other creatures as we go on our way to fulfill our Creator's holy designs.

3

Psalm 148 and Similar Prayers

In the last chapter, we explored how the Bible portrays animals helping humans on the way to salvation. In this chapter, we see that animals are intended to praise our Creator, right along with and beside us.

In the book of Psalms and elsewhere in the Bible, we find prayers in which human beings invite other creatures to praise God along with them. The clear impression in these prayers is that the nonhuman creatures are meant to participate in our prayerful journey into the presence of God. These are often very inclusive kinds of prayers addressed to a wide range of God's creation: sun and moon, trees, animals, birds, sea monsters, as well as to a variety of people.

Psalm 148 is a dramatic example of this. In the New American Bible (1986 edition), this psalm bears the awesome title: "Hymn of All Creation to the Almighty Creator." I invite you to read—or better, to pray—this hymn, which includes a broad spectrum of God's creatures:

PSALM 148

Hymn of All Creation to the Almighty Creator

I.   Praise the LORD from the heavens;
       praise him in the heights.
     Praise him, all you angels;
       praise him, all you his hosts.
     Praise him, sun and moon;
       praise him, all you shining stars.
     Praise him, you highest heavens,
       and you waters above the heavens.
     Let them praise the name of the LORD,
       for he commanded and they were created;
     He established them forever and ever;
       he gave them a duty which shall not pass away.

II. Praise the LORD from the earth,
       you sea monsters and all depths;
     Fire and hail, snow and mist,
       storm winds that fulfill his word;
     You mountains and all you hills,
       you fruit trees and all you cedars;
     You wild beasts and all tame animals,
       you creeping things and you winged foul.

III. Let the kings of the earth and all peoples,

    the princes and all the judges of the earth,

Young men too, and maidens,

    old men and boys,

Praise the name of the LORD,

    for his name alone is exalted;

His majesty is above earth and heaven,

    and he has lifted up the horn of his people.

Be this his praise from all his faithful ones,

    from the children of Israel, the people close to him.

Alleluia. (NAB 1986)

Several things strike me as I read these lines. First, we are told in the last two lines of the first stanza that God "commanded" these things—sun, stars, waters—"and they were created" just as in the creation story of Genesis. These few words of Psalm 148 seem clearly to be a wonderful echo of the first chapter of the Genesis story: God simply gives the word, and these creatures jump into existence. God says: "'Let there be light'; and there was light" (Genesis 1:3, NRSV) or "'let the dry land appear.' And it was so" (1:9) or "'Let the earth bring forth living creatures of every kind:' . . . And it was so" (1:24).

Then we are also told that God "established [all these creatures] forever and ever." To our ears, the text seems to suggest an eternal form of existence. But the people of the Old Testament did not seem to have a clear idea of eternity, at least in our sense of the term. For them, "forever and ever" could simply mean "a long time" or "throughout all time." With our Christian appreciation of a never-ending eternity, we readily see at least a hint in such passages of the continuation of nonhuman creatures into the world beyond. In fact, the next verse suggests no less than that when it asserts that God "gave them a duty [or role] *which shall not pass away*." Again, we have a hint in Sacred Scripture that these creatures will somehow continue their role of praising God, along with the human voices, in the world beyond.

It is also interesting to observe that in the first two stanzas, nonhuman creatures in heaven, sea, and earth are praising God. And in the final stanza, those praising God are all human beings. The picture we have, therefore, is that of the combined family of creation—humans and nonhumans—joined in praising God together. Doesn't that seem to be the way that God wills it? God is not seeking praise solely from the *human* part of the family of creation, but from the *whole* family of creation.

Just as in the story of the ark and the great flood, in which Noah and his family, along with the larger family of nonhuman creatures, are saved together, so it is in the case of this hymn in which all creatures are praising God together. *We are all in the same boat*, once again, seeking a share in God's mercy and love, and someday, final happiness in the restored garden.

Let me raise another interesting question regarding Psalm 148: where is the voice coming from in this hymn? In other words, who is inviting or encouraging all creatures to break out into this song of praise? This voice has to be coming from the rational creatures, from human beings who are the focus of the third part of the hymn. The last two lines of the hymn make this clear: "Be this his praise from all his faithful ones, from . . . the people close to him." In other words, the voice of this hymn is coming from God's faithful ones—God's *people*. These people are asking all creatures to accompany them in praising God. This may open up even greater possibilities for how we might relate to our animal companions.

For example, as mentioned in chapter 1, there are many places around the world where people of faith organize animal blessings. In these ceremonies, priests or other ministers ask God's blessing upon animals and other creatures. These creatures, in turn, are invited by their human companions to praise God. In chapter 7 you will read about one of the most amazing animal blessings in the world. It takes place each year on the feast of St. Francis inside the great Episcopal Cathedral of St. John the Divine in New York City. Perhaps the point of these blessings is that we should take their lessons and carry them with us in our everyday life.

Another way to answer the question of where the voice is coming from in Psalm 148 is to say that it is coming from worshipers in the temple. Singing hymns of praise to God was a familiar part of Israel's worship. In a symbolic way, we can say that all creation is praising God in a kind of cosmic temple where the whole family of creation is constantly at worship, singing God's praises. To carry the symbolism even further, we can imagine choirs singing "from the heavens" and "from the earth" in a form of stereophonic praise.

We turn now to a different setting, where another hymn of praise to God is sung by the three youths in the fiery furnace in the book of Daniel (chapter 3). In the midst of their distress, these three faithful youths (Hananiah, Azariah, and Mishael) voice this hymn inviting the whole family of creation to praise the one Lord of all.

I find it extremely interesting that Franciscan friar Thomas of Celano (1185–1260), a contemporary and a biographer of St. Francis, compared Francis's style of prayer to that of the three youths in the furnace. Immediately after referring specifically to the hymn of "the three youths in the fiery furnace," Celano says that Francis "never ceased to glorify, praise, and bless the Creator . . . in all the elements and creatures."[4] This certainly suggests to me that Francis was well aware of such hymns of praise in the Old Testament and would have undoubtedly modeled his own *Canticle of the Creatures* upon them. We will take a close look at Francis's canticle in the next chapter.

Meanwhile, here is a sampling of verses from the hymn, found in some Bibles, sung by the three youths in the furnace. Saved from the fire, they are singing out in one voice:

Bless the Lord, all you works of the Lord,
    praise and exalt him above all forever. . . .
Sun and moon, bless the Lord;
    praise and exalt him above all forever.
Stars of heaven, bless the Lord;
    praise and exalt him above all forever.
Every shower and dew, bless the Lord;
    praise and exalt him above all forever.
All you winds, bless the Lord;
    praise and exalt him above all forever.

Fire and heat, bless the Lord;

  praise and exalt him above all forever. . . .

Dew and rain, bless the Lord;

  praise and exalt him above all forever.

Frost and chill, bless the Lord;

  praise and exalt him above all forever.

Ice and snow, bless the Lord;

  praise and exalt him above all forever.

Nights and days, bless the Lord;

  praise and exalt him above all forever.

Light and darkness, bless the Lord;

  praise and exalt him above all forever.

Lightning and clouds, bless the Lord;

  praise and exalt him above all forever. . . .

Mountains and hills, bless the Lord;

  praise and exalt him above all forever. . . .

You springs, bless the Lord:

  praise and exalt him above all forever.

Seas and rivers, bless the Lord;

  praise and exalt him above all forever.

You dolphins and all water creatures, bless the Lord;

  praise and exalt him above all forever.

All you birds of the air, bless the Lord;

  praise and exalt him above all forever.

> All you beasts, wild and tame, bless the Lord;
>   praise and exalt him above all forever.
> You sons of men, bless the Lord;
>   praise and exalt him above all forever.
> (Daniel 3:57, 62–66, 68–82)

The hymn concludes with:

> Hananiah, Azariah, Mishael, bless the Lord;
>   praise and exalt him above all forever.
> For he has delivered us from the nether world,
>   and saved us from the power of death;
> He has freed us from the raging flame
>   and delivered us from the fire.
> Give thanks to the Lord for he is good,
>   for his mercy endures forever. (Daniel 3:88–89)

Again we have a picture of all creatures—both human and nonhuman—taking part in a prayer journey that concludes with all creatures praising God "above all forever" and giving "thanks to the Lord, for he is good." This word *good* takes us back to the first creation account in Genesis, where God looked upon all creatures and saw that they were "very good" (Genesis 1:31).

Let us consider one more example. The deuterocanonical book of Ben Sira (also known as Sirach or Ecclesiasticus) also reinforces the idea of God's goodness and the goodness of creation. As in the wisdom books in general, the writings of Ben Sira often dwell on the beauties of the created world. This is especially true of chapters 42 and 43. Though neither of these chapters uses the word *good* or *goodness*, they are permeated with the aura of God's beauty, glory, and holiness. Ben Sira's words (42:16) are a good example of this: "The sun looks down on everything with its light, and the work of the Lord is full of his glory" (NRSV).

Or consider this example: "The glory of the stars is the beauty of heaven, a glittering array in the heights of the Lord. On the orders of the Holy One they stand in their appointed places; they never relax in their watches. Look at the rainbow, and praise him who made it; it is exceedingly beautiful in its brightness. It encircles the sky with its glorious arc; the hands of the Most High have stretched it out" (Ben Sira 43:9–12, NRSV).

Or again, Ben Sira notes with eyes of wonder: "He scatters the snow like birds flying down, and its descent is like locusts alighting. The eye is dazzled by the beauty of its whiteness, and the mind is amazed as it falls" (Ben Sira 43:17–18, NRSV).

Ben Sira's poetic sense of awe and wonder and good-ness foreshadows the spirit of St. Francis, who believed that there is profound goodness in creatures because there is goodness in the Creator, and it simply overflows and passes into the goodness of creatures.

Although I mentioned earlier that Ben Sira did not actually utter the word *good* in chapters 42 or 43, he did utter the word loud and clear in chapter 39:16, where he introduced what became for him a kind of favorite statement or mantra: "The works of God are all of them good." He then repeated the statement with greater vigor in 39:32–33, saying: "So from the first I took my stand, and wrote down as my theme: The works of God are all of them good."

When the Bible refers to the created world as *good*, such as when God created the world in Genesis or in some of the passages above, the word *good* does not simply mean morally good. It also means "beautiful," as if reflecting the very "beauty" and "glory" of God. In Genesis, we see God smiling, as it were, like a happy artisan delighting in the work of creation, as if God is saying "Wow, that's beautiful! That's good!"

St. Francis often showed the same kind of delight as he enjoyed the gifts of creation in his native Italy. As St. Bonaventure, the great Franciscan mystic, pointed out more than once in the late thirteenth century, St. Francis saw in the beauty of a flower the One who is Beauty itself.

Psalm 104 conveys the same sense of awe, wonder, and beauty in response to the goodness of creation. In the New American Bible, the psalm bears the title "Praise of God the Creator." Here is a sampling of verses from another translation of that psalm, beginning at verse one:

Bless the Lord, O my soul!
   O Lord, my God, you are very great indeed.
You are clothed with honor and majesty,
   Wrapped in light as with a garment.
You stretch out the heavens like a tent,
   you set the beams of your chambers on the waters,
you make the clouds your chariot,
   you ride on the wings of the wind. . . .
You make springs gush forth in the valleys:
   They flow between the hills,
giving drink to every wild animal;
   the wild asses quench their thirst.
By the streams the birds of the air have their habitation;
   they sing among the branches.

From your lofty abode you water the mountains;
  the earth is satisfied with the fruit of your work.
You cause the grass to grow for the cattle,
  and plants for people to use,
to bring forth food from the earth,
  and wine to gladden the human heart.
oil to make the face shine,
  and bread to strengthen the human heart.
The trees of the Lord are watered abundantly,
  the cedars of Lebanon that he planted;
In them the birds build their nests;
  the stork has its home in the fir trees.
The high mountains are for the wild goats;
  the rocks are a refuge for coneys. . . .
May the glory of the Lord endure forever;
  may the Lord rejoice in his works.

(1–3, 10–18, 31, NRSV)

When we simply read (let alone pray) through the
psalms and other, related, biblical passages quoted in
this chapter, we cannot help noticing the intimate inter-
linking of Creator, humans, and other creatures: sun,
moon, stars, birds, animals, mountains, trees, streams,
and so forth. There is a growing sense that we truly are
one big family.

What these inspired biblical verses are suggesting to me is this: the whole family of creation is most happy when walking side by side in a common journey of praise toward the Creator who made us all. For those of you who already have great love for one or more animals, this will be no surprise—but perhaps you didn't realize how the Bible supported your sentiments. Can heaven be anything less than this: all of creation walking together?

4.

The Song of St. Francis

This is a perfect place to sketch out a fuller portrait of St. Francis of Assisi. The broad strokes of his life are familiar to most. St. Francis was born in 1182 in the Umbrian town of Assisi. The son of a prosperous cloth merchant, Francis was a carefree and generous youth. His companions dubbed him the "King of Revels." He loved the good life and partying with his friends. All the while, however, he dreamed of becoming a knight and achieving glory on the battlefield. The opportunity soon arrived and Francis road off as a knight of Assisi to fight against the neighboring town of Perugia.

Assisi, however, was roundly defeated in its very first skirmish and Francis was captured and became a prisoner of war. It was a bitter blow for this idealistic young man of twenty-one. Francis spent a year in prison and returned home to Assisi a broken man.

In time, however, Francis went off again as a knight in the papal army to battle the Holy Roman Emperor. But a short while later Francis received a message from God to go back to Assisi where he would find guidance regarding his future. Even though Francis feared he would be viewed by his friends and family as a coward, he returned in shame to his hometown.

Yet a plan seemed to be unfolding. While praying alone one day before a crucifix in the abandoned chapel of San Damiano located down the hill from Assisi, Francis heard these words coming from the cross: "Francis, repair my house, which is falling into ruin." The saint realized only later that it was a larger house, the Christian Church itself, that Christ was calling him to rebuild.

Another dramatic sign of Francis's new direction came through his meeting with a leper on the road. Francis was inspired to dismount his horse and warmly embrace and kiss the leper. Later Francis confessed in his *Testament* that "What had seemed bitter to me [an encounter with leprosy] was turned into sweetness of soul and body."[5] Francis realized that he had actually embraced his Lord, Jesus Christ.

Soon Francis found himself living among lepers and humbly caring for them. Others, seeing Francis joyfully ministering to the lepers and to other outcasts, asked to join Francis in his ministry to the poor. These followers would soon grow into a brotherhood, and in 1209, Pope Innocent III approved the Franciscan way of life.

But this early information about the life of St. Francis does not tell us about another very important aspect of Francis's life, namely his great admiration for the wonders of nature and the marvelous creatures that God placed on this earth to accompany us human creatures on our journey to God. This brings us directly to St. Francis's great *Canticle of the Creatures*. This hymn, or song of praise to our Creator, was composed very much in the spirit of Psalm 148 and the *Song of the Three Youths in the Fiery Furnace*, discussed in the previous chapter.

St. Francis, however, added a very personal touch to this song, also known as *The Canticle of Brother Sun*. He did this by giving the title of "Brother" and "Sister" to the various creatures addressed in his song, emphasizing as best he could his understanding that we all form *one family of creation* under one loving "Father" or Creator in heaven. "Sister" and "Brother," of course, are familial terms that people formerly only used for fellow humans.

Francis had a strong sense, which he probably learned from the Old Testament psalms and hymns, that we are not meant to journey to God alone, in proud isolation from our brother and sister creatures. Indeed, Francis would have regularly encountered these psalms and hymns in his liturgical prayers. For example, he would have certainly recited with frequency the following verses from the book of Daniel:

Sun and moon, bless the Lord;
    praise and exalt him above all forever.
Stars of heaven, bless the Lord;
    praise and exalt him above all forever.
Every shower and dew, bless the Lord;
    praise and exalt him above all forever.
All you winds, bless the Lord;
    praise and exalt him above all forever.
Fire and heat, bless the Lord;
    praise and exalt him above all forever. (3:62–66)

One can easily imagine Francis borrowing these words and phrases from the *Song of the Three Youths in the Fiery Furnace* and using them in his *Canticle of the Creatures*. Indeed, just as in the case of the psalms and hymns of the Hebrew Scriptures, Francis invites us in his exuberant *Canticle* to form one family with these creatures and to sing out in one symphony of praise to our common Creator. Here is a slightly condensed version of St. Francis's famous song:

The Canticle of the Creatures

Most high, all-powerful, all-good Lord!
>All praise is yours, all glory, all honor,
>and all blessing.
To you alone, Most High, do they belong.
>No mortal lips are worthy
>to pronounce your name.
All praise be yours, my Lord,
> through all that you have made,
And first my lord Brother Sun,
>who brings the day;
>and light you give to us through him.
>How beautiful is he,
>how radiant in all his splendor!
>Of you, Most High, he bears the likeness.

All praise be yours, my Lord,
   through Sister Moon and Stars,
      in the heavens you have made them, bright
      and precious and fair.
All praise be yours, my Lord,
   through Brothers Wind and Air,
      and fair and stormy, all the weather's moods,
      by which you cherish all that you have made.
All praise be yours, my Lord, through Sister Water,
   so useful, lowly, precious, and pure.
All praise be yours, my Lord, through Brother Fire,
   through whom you brighten up the night.
   How beautiful is he, how merry!
   Full of power and strength.
All praise be yours, my Lord,
   through Sister Earth, our mother,
      who feeds us in her sovereignty and produces
      various fruits and colored flowers and herbs. . . .
Praise and bless my Lord, and give him thanks,
   And serve him with great humility.[6]

Just as we find a spirit of great care and reverence for the creatures listed in St. Francis's *Canticle*, so we also find in Francis's daily life the same spirit of respect and reverence for every creature he encountered along his way.

Francis's care for creation even extended to earthworms he saw on the roadway. He would carefully pick them up and place them on the side of the road where they would be out of harm's way. Francis saw the goodness and beauty of God in the sunset or in a gurgling stream. He was in awe of the butterfly as well as the cricket. "Where the modern cynic sees something 'bug-like' in everything that exists," observed the German writer-philosopher Max Scheler, "St. Francis saw even in a bug the sacredness of life."

During his life, St. Francis had more than one mystical experience in which Jesus revealed himself as a God of overflowing goodness and love who would lay down his own life for Francis. The same incredible goodness that Francis saw in God he saw also in creatures. That is why he could compose a *Canticle of the Creatures* that not only praises the Creator as *good* in its opening line ("Most high, all-powerful, all-good Lord!") but also describes the creatures with similar words: "beautiful," "radiant," "bright," "precious and fair"—words shining with the glory and goodness of God.

Francis's amazement at God's goodness is reflected time and again in his style of prayer. In a prayer from his *Praises before the Office*, Francis suddenly begins repeating, if not babbling, the word *good*, as if intoxicated by it. He prays:

All powerful, all holy, most high and supreme God,
   sovereign good, all good,
   every good, you who alone
are good, it is to you we must give all praise,
   all glory, all thanks, all honor, all blessing;
   to you we must refer
   all good always. Amen.[7]

Artists, too, have often expressed this kind of goodness
and reverence in their artistic representations of St. Francis
and his fellow creatures. I think of the great painter Giotto
and his famous thirteenth-century fresco of *St. Francis
Preaching to the Birds* that is located in the Upper Basilica
of St. Francis in Assisi. In this painting, Francis and another
friar companion are standing in front of a tree and a large
group of birds are scattered on the ground before Francis
and looking intently toward him. Francis's right hand is
raised in blessing as he bends slightly before them in a
posture of gentle reverence, respect, and wonder before the
mystery of God's creation. The whole scene exudes a sense
of the presence and goodness of God—and the sacredness
of all God's creatures.

I think also of present-day artists who have sculpted
popular statues of St. Francis (some more elegant than
others) that stand in our flower gardens or on our bird

baths. I think also of greeting cards and T-shirts showing images of St. Francis with birds flying around his head or with a rabbit in his arms. Such images inspire us to love and respect all creatures.

To place Francis on a birdbath or in a rose garden or to show him with birds circling his head is simply a popular way of saying that this little man had a special link with all God's creatures, and it's just like him to be standing humbly among them or leaning over to show them care and respect. St. Francis would claim that the birds coming to the birdbath are holy. Water is holy and good, and so are all God's creatures.

For Francis, the *whole* created world was holy—not something evil to be rejected. Francis made all things into a sacred ladder by which he could ascend to his Creator, as St. Bonaventure and other thirteenth-century biographers often noted. Is not his *Canticle of the Creatures* a wonderful example of this kind of "ladder," inviting creatures upward and closer to God?

The Catholic bishops of the United States published a document in 1992 entitled *Renewing the Earth*. In it the bishops praised St. Francis and emphasized: "Safeguarding creation requires us to live responsibly in it, rather than managing creation as though we are outside it."[8] We should see ourselves, they added, as stewards within creation, not as separated from it. In this, Francis was certainly ahead of his time. He saw himself, as do today's environmentalists, as part of the ecosystem, not as a proud master over and above it.

St. Francis addressed creatures as "sisters" and "brothers," that is, as equals, not as subjects to be dominated. That is why the humble figure of St. Francis standing on the birdbath or among the shrubs is so right for our day. He truly saw himself as a simple servant and a caretaker of creation—little brother to the birds and the fish and the lowly ivy.

For these reasons and more, Pope John Paul II proclaimed St. Francis of Assisi the patron of ecology in 1979. The pope cited him for being "an example of genuine and deep respect for the integrity of creation." "St. Francis," he added, "invited all creation—animals, plants, natural forces, even Brother Sun and Sister Moon—to give honor and praise to the Lord."

There are many other popular stories about St. Francis in which he showed respect for animals and other creatures. Here are a few of them:

One day a rabbit was brought to him by a brother who had found it caught in a trap. Francis admonished the rabbit to be more careful in the future. Releasing the rabbit from the trap, Francis sat it on the ground and told it to go its way. But the rabbit just hopped back to Francis and sat on his lap, desiring to stay close to him. Francis carried the rabbit into the woods and set it free. The rabbit simply followed Francis back to where he was seated and jumped onto his lap again. Finally Francis asked one of his brothers to take the rabbit deep into the forest and let it go. This time it worked; the rabbit remained content there. Such episodes were always happening to Francis, who saw this as an opportunity to give praise to God.

Francis also made friends with fish. Once, he was crossing a lake with a fisherman, who caught a nice-sized fish and gave it to Francis as a gift. Francis, however, simply warned the fish not to get caught again and placed it back in the water. The fish remained in the water near the boat until Francis gave it permission to leave. Only then did it swim off to freedom. Francis, being in tune with animals and other creatures and having a great respect for them, had an instinctual closeness to them, and whether he communicated with them by words or not, is not so important as his great love and sensitivity on their behalf.

This brings us to the well-known legend of Francis and a fierce wolf that had been terrorizing the Italian village of Gubbio. The wolf had attacked and even killed some of the townspeople, including children. Through the intervention of Francis, the vicious killing ceased and the wolf and townspeople made peace with each other. The townspeople promised to feed the wolf, if the wolf stopped its violent attacks. Francis brought the conflict between the townspeople and the wolf to a peaceful solution. He was the sort of person—extraordinarily rare but possible—who could communicate with creatures, because he was sensitive to them and to their needs.

Finally we have the famous story of Francis's preaching to the birds. Sometimes people hear this story out of its proper context. This episode was not a fanciful event where Francis preached a heartfelt sermon to a big flock of birds. We shouldn't make it into something magical, unrelated to real life. The story, however, can catch us off guard. We think it is going in one direction, but it takes a turn in quite a different direction.

In reading the story again recently, I was puzzled by where Francis's biographer St. Bonaventure positioned this famous story in his *Life of St. Francis*. He placed the story right at the point in Francis's life where he is struggling with a deep personal dilemma: should he retire from the world and devote himself entirely to prayer, or should he continue traveling about as a preacher of the

gospel? To answer this question, St. Francis sent brothers to seek the advice of two of Francis's most trusted
colleagues: Brother Sylvester and the holy virgin Clare
and her sisters.

The word came back very quickly from both Sylvester
and Clare that it was their clear judgment that God wanted
Francis to keep proclaiming the Good News of God's saving
love. No sooner did Francis hear their response than he
immediately stood up, and in the words of St. Bonaventure,
"without the slightest delay he took to the roads to carry
out the divine command" with great fervor.[9]

The typical reader at this juncture, I believe, would
expect St. Bonaventure to portray Francis as running off
to the nearest village or marketplace to begin preaching
the gospel to the people gathered there. But where does
Francis actually go? Francis's very next stop, according
to Bonaventure, is this: "He came to a spot where a large
flock of birds of various kinds had come together. When
God's saint saw them, he quickly ran to the spot and
greeted them as if they were endowed with reason. . . ."

He went right up to them and solicitously urged them
to listen to the word of God, saying,

> "Oh birds, my brothers [and sisters], you have a
> great obligation to praise your Creator, who clothed

you in feathers and gave you wings to fly with, provided you with pure air and cares for you without any worry on your part. . . ." The birds showed their joy in a remarkable fashion: They began to stretch their necks, extend their wings, open their beaks, and gaze at him attentively.

He went through their midst with amazing fervor of spirit, brushing against them with his tunic. Yet none of them moved from the spot until the man of God made the sign of the cross and gave them permission to leave; then they all flew away together. His companions waiting on the road saw all these things. When he returned to them, that pure and simple man began to accuse himself of negligence because he had not preached to the birds before.[10]

Thomas of Celano, who wrote an earlier biography of St. Francis, told this same story of St. Francis's sermon to the birds, including Francis's admission of "negligence," but Celano adds these significant details: "From that day on, [Francis] solicitously admonished all birds, all animals and reptiles, and even creatures that have no feeling, to praise and love their Creator. . . . "[11]

I must say that Bonaventure's version of the story was a great shock to me. Had not Francis just learned from his special advisors Brother Sylvester and Lady Clare that God wanted him to continue his preaching minis-try? Should we not assume that the primary audience of his preaching should be other human beings—and not a large flock of birds? I believe that Bonaventure is trying to shock us into widening our horizons, and into learning with St. Francis that the whole family of creation deserves more respect and ought to be invited to praise God along with us human beings. Maybe just as Francis accused himself of negligence for not inviting the birds—and other animals, reptiles, and so forth—to praise God with him, so we, too, need to admit the same kind of negligence.

The more Francis grew in wisdom and in his under-standing that God's saving love goes out to all creatures, the more he saw that all creatures—not just humans—make up the full family of creation. Francis was keenly aware that God created everything out of love and that God ultimately wants all creatures to share in that same love forever. As we grow in our awareness of God's great love for each and every creature, you and I should all the more consciously be inviting every creature to join us in praising our Creator.

The basic question being asked by this book is this: will we see our animal companions and the rest of God's creatures in heaven? We have seen in this chapter how St. Francis—in imitation of Psalm 148 and the *Song of the Three Youths in the Fiery Furnace*—has invited all creatures to join him in praising God *here on earth*.

Wouldn't it seem strange if our sister and brother creatures —who have been invited, in each of these songs, to praise God with us here in this life—are not welcome to praise God with us *in heaven?* I think God would surely find something contradictory about this.

Jesus and the World of Creation

5

Jesus of Nazareth, of course, lived his earthly life twelve centuries before St. Francis of Assisi. Indeed, long before Francis understood a sense of brotherhood with the rest of creation, Jesus, the eternal Word of God, had plunged in and immersed himself in the created world, becoming a *brother to every creature*. This he did through the Incarnation—a breathtaking event that sent rumblings of new life and hope through the entire network of creation.

The Incarnation is the central mystery of Christianity. One thing is very clear: Jesus, as the Divine Word, did not hold himself aloof from the world he had come to save, but literally and wholeheartedly *entered* the family of creation. He did this through his incarnation, his taking human form, his birth at Bethlehem. It's an amazing mystery, because when the Word became flesh in Christ and made his home among us, not only were human beings raised to a new and glorious dignity but also all other creatures as well.

This is the wonder of Christ's incarnation: it leads us to a deeper understanding of not only our own heightened dignity as human beings, but also the heightened dignity of each of our brother and sister creatures.

When Jesus walked this earth as the Word made flesh, he must have perceived very acutely that the whole world had been greatly ennobled by his entering into it. Therefore, why wouldn't Jesus interact and intermingle with the earth in a most natural and comfortable way, with a profound regard for his own dignity and the goodness of all created things? As a matter of fact, Jesus felt at home on this earth, whether on the lakeshore or in the desert, whether walking down a mountainside or crossing a wheat field or sailing across the Sea of Galilee.

In his preaching of the Good News of God's saving love, Jesus delighted in using images from nature, such as the birds of the air and the lilies of the field. He naturally populated his sermons with stories of foxes, pearls, salt, yeast, fig trees, mustard seed, weeds and wheat, moths, and lost sheep. He certainly understood from his profound knowledge of Scripture that all these creatures were blessed and pronounced *good* by the Creator in the beginning.

Jesus used many created things in his saving work, such as wet clay to heal the eyes of a blind man (John 9:6–7). He used bread and wine, the product of wheat and grapes, to represent his very presence in the Eucharist. We see from examples like this how Jesus incorporated other creatures into his own mission of carrying out God's saving plan for the world. We saw earlier signs of this in the story of Noah and the ark, where the dove helped Noah to bring to safety all creatures living in the ark. Throughout biblical literature, we have seen many instances of human beings and other creatures cooperating together—as one big family of creation—to advance God's saving mission.

Finally, near the end of Mark's Gospel, in his farewell message to his disciples, Jesus left a strong hint that the whole family of creation was to be included in God's saving work. After his death and resurrection, Jesus tells his disciples: "Go into the whole world and proclaim the gospel to every creature" (Mark 16:15). Mark does not use the words "to every human being," but "to every creature." Jesus' choice of words suggests that he knows that the gospel message will have a saving impact upon the *whole* family of creation, and not simply on the human family.

Stopping by Assisi, Where Francis Called the Sun His "Brother"

In the summer of 1973, I returned from an assignment in the Philippines as a teacher of literature in a Franciscan seminary and college near Manila. On my trip back to Cincinnati, I had the opportunity to stay for several days in Assisi, the birthplace of St. Francis. At the time, I was already pondering the question, mentioned several times already in this book: why was St. Francis always addressing his fellow creatures as Brother Sun, Sister Moon, Sister Water, Brother Fire, and so forth? It was in this very part of Italy that St. Francis so frequently addressed his fellow creatures as "brothers" and "sisters." Here he composed his *Canticle of the Creatures*. It dawned on me more and more clearly that Francis had come to understand, indeed, that all creatures formed *one family of creation*.

Something about Assisi and the life of St. Francis helped bring this favorite theme of mine into sharper focus. It was not long after this first visit to Assisi that I wrote the following lines. Apparently, my conviction that we are not wise to separate ourselves from the larger family of creation had already taken root in my soul.

> You and I spend everyday of our lives
>   amid trees, wind, insects and seashells,
>   hardly aware of the integral link
>   we have with them.
> We often assume a stance of aloofness toward them,
>   not knowing how closely related we really are.
> We breathe the sky into our lungs
>   and rely each moment on the sun's warmth.

We feed daily on plants, animals, and minerals.
 The calcium in our teeth once belonged to
 shellfish living below us in prehistoric seas.
Our blood stream is inverted ocean water—
 its tides still influenced by the moon.
It's not Francis who is odd for
 calling the sun his brother,
  But we for not doing so.
Unlike Francis, we have grown estranged
 from our environment,
  and we drive it farther away by our irreverence
  and constant pollutings.

These reflective lines are simply an attempt to suggest that we are "brothers" and "sisters" to every other creature in the universe. In other words, all creatures, human and nonhuman alike, make up one vast family of creation.

To follow in the footsteps of St. Francis is to have a renewed understanding of Christ and his relationship to the created world. In the Franciscan way of looking at things, Jesus, the Word made flesh, is not simply a part of creation. Rather, Christ is the *final goal and destination* toward which all creation is headed. A key point of the Franciscan view, surprising to some, is this: the

Word of God did not become a creature and a human being because of Adam and Eve's sin. On the contrary, the Divine Word became flesh because from all eternity God wanted Christ to be creation's most perfect work, the model and crown of creation and of humanity. According to the Franciscan view, the Word would have come and entered our created world, even if Adam and Eve had not sinned.

The foremost champion of these views was the Franciscan friar John Duns Scotus. John Scotus was born in Scotland in 1266, only forty years after the death of St. Francis. He was educated in England's Oxford University and ordained a Franciscan priest in 1291. He taught theology at the University of Paris; from there he went to teach in Cologne, Germany, where he died in 1308 at age forty-two.

The approach of Blessed John Duns Scotus may differ at times from what we may think to be standard Catholic theology. Yet his theological views have never been labeled unacceptable by the church. In fact, some saw in the beatification of John Duns Scotus by Pope John Paul II in 1993 a belated vote of confidence in his holiness and virtue, as well as in the value of his theological contributions. Over the centuries, most Franciscans have happily embraced Scotus's way of looking at Christ and the world of creation.

Duns Scotus's viewpoint, moreover, has gained greater prominence in recent times. His view of the created world, for example, is reflected in the work of the great nineteenth-century Jesuit poet Gerard Manley Hopkins—in poems such as "God's Grandeur," "The Windhover," and "Pied Beauty." Scotus's ideas have also shown up in the spiritual writings of Trappist monk Thomas Merton, and in those of the Jesuit priest-anthropologist Pierre Teilhard de Chardin.

"Christ is not an afterthought in the divine plan," writes de Chardin. "He is the Alpha and the Omega, the beginning and the end of all things."[12]

According to Scotus's teaching, God's first intention—from all eternity—was that human nature be glorified by being united with the Divine Word. This was to happen *regardless* of Adam and Eve's innocence or sinfulness. To say that the Incarnation of Christ was simply an *afterthought* of God, dependent on Adam's fall, would be to base the rich Christian theology of the Incarnation on sin. This did not make sense to Duns Scotus. Christ, the Word made flesh, was intended by God from all eternity to be the crown and goal of creation and not simply some kind of Plan B arrangement, or "last-minute cure," to offset the sin of Adam and Eve.

Of course, given humanity's disobedience, the *way* Jesus Christ came was, in fact, in the form of a Savior whose great act of overflowing love and forgiveness set us free. In Scotus's view, however, the Divine Word would have entered creation and human history under any circumstances, as the perfect model of the fully alive human being. It was not Adam who served as the blueprint or pattern for the humanity of Christ: it was the other way around. According to Scotus, Jesus Christ was the blueprint or model in God's mind for creating Adam and Eve and the rest of humankind.

The followers of St. Francis were not the first proponents of these ideas. The letters of the great apostle St. Paul had already given the world a solid basis for seeing Christ as the pattern and summit of all creation. Indeed, Paul teaches that in God's eternal plan, before the world was made, God the Father had already decided to send the Divine Word as the perfect model for humanity.

As Paul spells out in the letter to the Ephesians, "[God the Father] chose us in him [Jesus Christ], before the foundation of the world, to be holy and without blemish before him" (Ephesians 1:4). A few verses later, Paul adds that part of God's saving plan was "to sum up all things in Christ, in heaven and on earth" (Ephesians 1:10).

Then, in his Letter to the Colossians, we read Paul's most celebrated passage about what many of us call the *Primacy of Christ*, that is, Christ's holding *preeminence* or *first place* among all creatures:

> [Christ] is the image of the invisible God,
>   the firstborn of all creation.
> For in him were created all things in heaven
>   and on earth,
>   the visible and invisible,
>   all things were created through him and for him.
> He is before all things
>   and in him all things hold together.
>   (Colossians 1:15–17)

At St. Francis Capuchin College in Washington, DC, there is an attractive nine-foot tall painting called the *Primacy of Christ*, by Sister Mary Thomas, a Franciscan nun and artist who lives at a Poor Clare Monastery in Cleveland, Ohio. In this painting we see an imposing head-to-foot image of the risen and glorified Christ, dressed mainly in garments of red.

But covering most of Christ's chest and midsection is a cubistic swirl of humans (on top) with hands reaching out in praise, and below them in the same swirl are many other creatures: a giraffe, horses, tigerlike animals, birds, fish and other sea and reptilelike creatures, fruit trees rooted in Mother Earth, ears of corn, flowers, a bunch of grapes, and vegetation, along with a luminous sun and planets.

When I interviewed Sister Mary Thomas, she revealed to me that her painting is an artistic expression of Scotus's teaching about Christ being first in all things, as well as "the goal of creation." The painting is also a reflection on the passage from Colossians quoted above (1:15–17), especially the words: "In him were created all things" (1:16) and "He is before all things, and in him all things hold together" (1:17).

Keeping this same painting of the "primacy of Christ" in mind, we see how similar themes are also expressed in the first lines of the prologue of St. John's Gospel:

In the beginning was the Word,
  and the Word was with God,
  and the Word was God.
He was in the beginning with God.
All things came to be through him,
  and without him nothing came to be.
  (John 1:1–3)

Most Franciscans, I believe, have in one way or another embraced this vision. And you who desire to follow Francis in a closer understanding of the human relationship to creation may want to do this, as well. Whether conscious of it or not, we are inclined to see all created things as pieces of a beautiful puzzle that makes sense only when fitted into a larger framework—the image of Christ.

"There is nothing in this world that makes sense apart from Jesus Christ," says Father Stephen Doyle, OFM, a well-known Franciscan Scripture scholar and popular preacher. "Whatever exists in this world was made for the sake of Jesus Christ." A bit later he grows more poetic: "If we looked around and listened to the world about us, and if the singing birds could be formed into a chorus and the rustling breeze and tinkling rain could have a voice, and the roar of the ocean could be put into words, they would all have one thing to say: 'We were made for the sake of Jesus Christ.'"[13]

Father Stephen also offers a good solution to the riddle: how can Christ, who came *after* Adam and Eve, come *before* them in the mind of God? How can the incarnate Word of God be first and last at the same time? In providing an answer, he borrows from a popular explanation given by St. Francis de Sales in his *Treatise on the Love of God*:

If you wanted to make wine, what would you do? First of all, you would have to plant a vineyard. Then you would have to fertilize the vines. You would have to trim them. Eventually, you would harvest the grapes, press them, and let them ferment. Finally, you would get some wine.

What was the first thing on your mind? The wine.

What was the last thing you got? The wine.

In the same way, notes Father Stephen, Jesus' arriving late on the scene does not contradict his holding first place in God's mind at the creation of the universe. Christ is the first and the last, the Alpha and the Omega.

In the ongoing process of creation and in human history itself, there are many elements: minerals, plants, animals, human characters. In the Christian view, as St. Paul expresses it so well, all these elements and characters come to a culmination in Jesus Christ. God's plan, as we know, is "to sum up all things in Christ, in heaven and on earth" (see Ephesians 1:10). I don't think we should separate Christ's story from our own story. Nor can we separate our human story from that of the minerals, plants, and other nonhuman creatures that have participated in shaping our story.

As Scripture professor Father Michael Guinan, OFM, of the Franciscan School of Theology in Berkeley,

California, recently related to me, "Modern science is showing so clearly how we—in our whole bodies—are tightly bound to the 'stuff of the universe.' We are literally made of stardust!"

Consider the metaphor of a stage play, where what happens on that stage is a shadowy image of what happens in our real lives. Similarly, what happens in our own small lives, and the lives of every creature on earth, is in the end, part of the larger drama of God's history itself.

Let us extend this metaphor even further: when the curtains reopen or the lights come up again at the end of a play, we once again see the familiar set and furnishings of that play, the "world" of the drama just presented. All the characters, from the lesser to the greater, begin coming on to the stage. All have been part of this one dramatic story, this "one word" or "conception" expressing the mind and heart of the author. One by one, the performers continue to fill up the stage until at the very end, as the lights grow brighter and the applause grows stronger, the star of the show—glowing in the light—comes forward to take a bow.

We can look at the drama of history and salvation in a similar way. All of us humans, along with our fellow creatures, over the centuries have been offered a role to play in the drama—a drama we can call *Word Becoming*

Flesh. When the drama ends, we all have a chance to take our little bows and then turn to await the reentrance of the lead player, Jesus Christ, the head and summit of all creation.

As the perfect model of all creation walks back onto the stage to take his final bow, the lights grow brighter, and the shouts of praise from the whole audience of creation are a most beautiful sound.

St. Francis and the Incarnation

6

As we have seen, the mystery of God's entering the family of creation, as a human child named Jesus, had an enormous impact on the life and teachings of St. Francis. In some way or another, the mystery of the Incarnation struck his imagination like a flash of lightning. Something made Francis realize that when the Word entered the world of creation and became flesh, everything was changed—profoundly and forever.

It's as though the very dust of the earth was transformed through God's entrance into the created universe. Did not John the Baptist proclaim in the words of Isaiah that "all flesh shall see the salvation of God" (Luke 3:6)? As experts in the study of the Hebrew Scriptures will tell you, when a Hebrew author makes a statement such as "*all flesh* shall see the salvation of God," the expression *all flesh* can apply not only to humans but also to animals and other creatures.

For example, God tells Noah, "I am going to bring a flood of waters on the earth, to destroy from under heaven all flesh in which is the breath of life: everything that is on earth shall die" (Genesis 6:17, NRSV). Further on, God tells Noah of his plan to save representatives of all flesh by way of the ark: "Of every living thing, of all flesh," God says, "you shall bring two of every kind into the ark, to keep them alive with you" (Genesis 6:19). In this case, God is not talking about only the human inhabitants of the ark, but "two of every kind" of the "birds" and "animals" and "every creeping thing of the ground" (see 6:20).

Francis's sense of kinship with the created world was closer to the Hebrew outlook than to that of the Greek philosophers. According to many Greek thinkers, *spirit* is what makes for unity. These Greek thinkers believed that it is *matter* that divides. In their view, all individuals partake of one world spirit. It is my unique chunk of matter, however, that makes me different from you and imprisons my portion of the world spirit. When I die, my soul, freed from its (material) prison, sails back into the one spirit. In dissolving into this sea of unity, I lose my individuality. So the Greek way of thinking goes.

This Greek view is neither the Hebrew perspective nor that of St. Francis. From both the Hebrew perspective and that of Francis, *flesh* is a unifier, not a divider. Flesh makes for kinship, unity, and continuity. For example, one Hebrew kinsman says to another: "This at last is bone of my bones and flesh of my flesh" (Genesis 2:23, NRSV). We learn elsewhere in Genesis that husband and wife "become one flesh" (2:24). Jesus repeats the same idea when he says, ". . . a man shall leave his father and mother and be joined to his wife, and the two shall become one flesh" (Matthew 19:5, NRSV). Flesh can also be viewed more broadly as the whole fabric of creation, as when the psalmist invites us to "give thanks to the Lord, . . . who gives food to all flesh" (see Psalm 136:1, 25, NRSV).

St. Francis saw the world of flesh in the same way. He knew from the stories in the book of Genesis that there is one stuff or material from which all things are made and which unifies all things. Genesis 2:9–19, for example, portrays God as making all earthly things—minerals, plants, trees, animals, birds, human beings—from the same basic matter (soil, clay, dust). Yes, as the psalmist informs us, "[God] knows how we were made; he remembers that we are dust" (Psalm 103:14, NRSV).

Francis was keenly aware of that one moment in history that we call the Incarnation. At that moment God entered creation as the Word was made flesh. For Francis, that event sent spiritual vibrations through the whole network of dust and flesh. Not only was human nature made holy by the Incarnation, but also the whole fabric of creation was charged with the divine presence.

This is why the mystery of the Incarnation and the feast of Christmas meant so much to St. Francis, and why he fervently believed that all creatures should take part in this feast. As is well known, history credits Francis with promoting the popular tradition of the Christmas crib or crèche. The custom goes back to the year 1223, when he invited the townspeople of Greccio, Italy, to come to a cave outside of town and reenact the first Christmas.

Francis instructed the people to bring an ox and an ass and sheep with them and to have real straw in a real manger. Legend tells us that the Christ child appeared in the straw, and Francis held the infant in his arms. The Gospel of St. Luke mentions that Mary laid Jesus in a manger, but there is no mention in the Gospels of an ox and an ass. Some see in Isaiah 1:3 a hint of this:

> An ox knows its owner,
> and an ass, its master's manger;
> But Israel does not know. . . .

But sometimes it's tradition that accounts for additions to the biblical story, and Francis was either honoring a tradition of animals, or simply adding to tradition. Either way, it makes for a beautiful rendering of that eventful moment in history. Most of all, Francis sensed that, by right, all creatures should participate in the celebration of Christmas. He saw how fitting it was to have an ox and an ass present in that humble cave.

Francis's biographers go even further. They tell us that in order to extend the feast to all creatures, Francis wanted the emperor to instruct all people to scatter grain along the roads on Christmas day so that the birds and other animals would have plenty to eat for the feast. The beasts in the stables, too, should be given finer fare and even the walls should be rubbed with good food.

I believe that many of us have the same instinct as St. Francis, though we may be only vaguely aware of it. We, too, seek to include the whole family of creation in our celebration of Christmas. Consider for a moment our Christmas tree custom. What do we do? We go out to the countryside (or, more likely, to the supermarket) and get a tree. We bring this obvious symbol of the creature-world into our living rooms and churches and decorate it beautifully as Christmas approaches, covering it with strings of lights and lots of ornaments or tinsel. Some of us also decorate our trees and shrubs—even our houses—with lights.

Unconsciously are we not bringing "Brother Tree," "Sister Light," and other parts of our created world into the celebration of Christ's incarnation and birth? If Francis were alive today, he would no doubt encourage us to include more and more creatures in our Christmas celebration. He might even suggest that we put bright ribbons on "Brother Dog" and "Sister Cat." Or we could serve all our pets special treats on Christmas day, or at least toss a few more sunflower seeds on the bird feeder.

Our growing respect for all God's creatures, based on our deepening understanding of the Incarnation, should not be restricted to Christmas day. Our days will be richly blessed if we carry this new awareness of the sacredness of all creatures with us every day of the year. Those of us in the Judeo-Christian tradition already know of the goodness of all creation from the creation accounts of

Genesis. We believe that our Creator, a God of overflowing goodness, has transmitted this goodness into the whole created world and has repeatedly affirmed that the created world is *good*.

This leads many of us to accept what we call the principle of sacramentality. This is the belief that every created thing can be a sign or sacrament or reflection of the divine. In other words, all creatures can convey or mediate the presence of God for us.

The blessing of animals, which is growing quite popular among people of all backgrounds and denominations around the world, is a vivid expression of this sacramentality. This custom of blessing animals is surely a way of paying respect to the sacredness and goodness of creatures. It's also a way of saying that pets and animals and other creatures are already richly blessed by God. Our animal-blessing ceremonies are simply a way of saying yes to the blessedness and sacredness that already exists in creatures.

For over fifteen years at St. Boniface Church in the heart of San Francisco, a Franciscan friar has blessed animals on the feast of St. Francis. "I started the blessings eight years ago," Father Floyd Lotito told me several years ago. "And I get phone calls from people throughout the year. 'When's it going to be?' they ask. 'My dog is sick. Can you bless my dog?'"

"I love doing the blessing. It's a wonderful thing," says the friendly friar who resides at the friary next to the church. "I like sharing St. Francis's vision with people. St. Francis saw all creatures as being in harmony—as one family. And so he could address them as Brother Sun, Sister Moon, Brother Dog, and Sister Cat."

During the hours of the blessing, the San Francisco police as a courtesy block off Golden Gate Avenue in front of the church. When I was there, a policeman's horse seemed to like Fr. Floyd, especially when the friar walked onto the street and gave the horse a preliminary blessing by sprinkling it with water. The horse began calmly nibbling on the sleeve of Fr. Floyd's brown Franciscan habit as the friar stood there, smiling.

The blessing ceremony actually started, however, in the courtyard of St. Clare in front of the church and friary, which had been adorned with colorful balloons and streamers. Fr. Floyd wore a decorated stole and a festive lei of flowers over his brown habit. At times he donned a San Francisco Giants baseball cap to keep the bright sun out of his eyes.

When it came time to bless the animals, the friar gave a short talk from a small raised platform. "Peace and every blessing!" he said to the guests. "Thank you for coming and bringing your pets." With a smile, he looked at the people scattered about the courtyard, some carrying pets in their arms, others controlling them with leashes.

"October fourth," the friar continued, "is the feast of St. Francis, the patron of our city and the patron saint of ecology. St. Francis was a lover, a peacemaker, a unifier, a bridge. There are stories of St. Francis blessing the birds; a frightened, trapped rabbit; the fish—and of his making peace between a fierce wolf and the town of Gubbio."

As Fr. Floyd spoke, some of the pets sat quietly, as if listening to the friar. At other times, however, skirmishes broke out as excited dogs barked and snarled at each other until they were subdued by their caretakers. As a rule, cats were quieter—some extremely nervous after discovering that they were outnumbered by dogs. They sometimes wailed their terror or displeasure from the safety of cardboard containers.

With a warm, cordial voice, Fr. Floyd went on peacefully: "St. Francis saw all creation: humanity, animals, the environment, plants, trees, the flowers, sun, moon, stars, water, wind, air—all the earth—as good brothers and sisters, revealing God's love, providence, and beauty to us."

"The way you respect creation, our mother earth, the way you treat animals, reflects the way you treat others. When you care for the earth and the animals, it makes you a better person, a kinder person," the friar said as he ended his talk. "Now let us bless the animals."

In a strong voice, Father Floyd first said a general blessing: "Blessed are you, Lord God, maker of all living creatures. You inspired St. Francis to call all animals his brothers and sisters. We ask you to bless these animals by the power of your love, enable them to live according to your plan. May we always praise you for all your beauty in creation. Blessed are you, Lord our God, in all your creatures. Amen."

Father Floyd gave another blessing for animals that were sick: "Heavenly Father, you created all things for your glory and called us to treat lovingly the animals under our care. We ask you to restore these creatures to health and strength. Blessed are you, Lord God, and holy is your name for ever and ever. Amen."

Then the friar invited the people to bring their pets forward to be blessed individually. As they presented their pets to Fr. Floyd, he asked them for the names of the animals so he could bless them by name. One by one, he sprinkled holy water and gently placed his hand on each of them.

"Lars, my friend, God bless you," the friar said cheerfully to small pug-faced dog, one of the three Chinese pugs present for the ceremony. "Stay in good health,

Cotton," he pronounced softly to a white rabbit held in a young woman's arms. So it went until all were blessed.

Though most of the pets were dogs and cats, there were others creatures also, including a parakeet in a cage and a guinea pig with a wriggling nose. The *San Francisco Examiner* reported on the blessing in the next day's paper with two photos and a story headlined: "Pets Receive Blessing of St. Francis: Father Lotito Greets Animals by Name."

"Over the years," the article noted, "Father Floyd has blessed iguanas, ferrets, stuffed animals, pictures of animals, ashes of animals. He even bestows a special blessing by phone each year on Fat Albert, a parrot who wasn't suppose to live very long," but who still survives after many blessings.[14]

Fr. Floyd is a well-known personality in San Francisco. For years, he has been a fixture at "St. Anthony Dining Room" and at other programs sponsored by the Franciscan friars for the poor and homeless near St. Boniface. Fr. Floyd is a native of Los Angeles and the son of immigrant Italian parents. He has served the street people of San Francisco for over forty years, especially in the "Tenderloin" district that surrounds St. Boniface Church.

His blessings of animals have received wide media coverage. The event has been featured on local and national TV news, and has even gone international on CNN. But what message does Fr. Floyd hope to convey to the public through his annual blessing of the animals? I asked him.

"Mainly that God is good and gracious and wonderful," replies the friar. "God loves us in a very unrestricted and inclusive way. God's care extends beyond the human family to the whole family of creation. All creation is good. There is no dichotomy between the secular and the sacred. God loves all creatures. I feel that strongly!"

Now seventy-four, Father Floyd assures me that, although he has slowed down a bit, the annual animal blessing is still popular and, since 2006, he has been holding the blessings inside the church. "People still come in good numbers," he says, "and now they can attend Mass alongside their pets." The blessings are done after Mass, and the whole event still gets media attention. But, of course, the purpose of animal blessings in churches is not only to spread the word about God's love and care for our animal companions, but also to honor the ways that God is blessing our pets and animals all of the time, even in ways that we may find hard to imagine.

Praying with Creatures

7.

Coming as I do from the Roman Catholic tradition, my fellow worshipers and I are used to liturgies of prayer that rely heavily on a very wide and rich spectrum of creatures. On our most solemn feasts, for example, we use fire, clouds of incense, blazing candles, and multicolored flowers. In our sacramental celebrations, we use bread, wine, water, oil, ashes, and palm branches. We decorate our prayer spaces with stained glass windows, images of lambs, doves, lions, eagles,

oxen, and asses. We pray in the company of these creatures day after day in our public worship.

As a Catholic I find it very normal to incorporate these
brother and sister creatures into my worship of God.
Being a member of the Franciscan family makes it all the
more natural. Surely, what I described in the last chapter
as the principle of sacramentality is very much the air we
breathe, whether it is a matter of celebrating the Eucharist
or other sacraments or public prayers that mention our
fellow creatures. Christians of all backgrounds can believe
in the inherent holiness and sanctity of all these creatures,
accepting them as outward signs and "sacraments" of
God's presence, goodness, and grace.

A whole area of liturgical prayer that has not been
mentioned above is the use of music or what we can
call "sound creatures." We often forget the wide variety
of created things used in worship that rely on music
and sound. This idea is by no means new. Think of the
many worshipers praising God with the help of musical
instruments in the Hebrew Scriptures. Psalm 150 is a
good example of this. In the New American Bible, the
title given for Psalm 150 is "Final Doxology with Full
Orchestra"—this orchestra, we might note, includes
three sections: wind, strings, and percussion. In slightly
condensed form, the psalm reads:

Praise God in his holy sanctuary. . . .
Give praise with blasts upon the horn,
  praise him with harp and lyre,
Give praise with tambourines and dance,
  praise him with flutes and strings,
Give praise with crashing cymbals.
  praise him with sounding cymbals.
Let everything that has breath
  give praise to the LORD!
Hallelujah! (1a, 3–6)

Christian worship is often enriched by the presence of musical instruments or "sound-making creatures" such as those found in Psalm 150. Think of musical instruments made of earthly materials like metal, wood, ivory, bamboo, and so on. Singing music accompanied by a wide assortment of instruments is a common experience in a variety of Christian churches today, and, of course, we have moved beyond the instruments mentioned in the Bible. I think, for example, of choral groups accompanied by keyboard, guitars, drums, or maybe even tambourines, trumpets, or saxophones. These "creatures" made of earthly materials assist the choral group and congregation as they lift their voices in praise to God.

Even in simple ceremonies today where Christian wor-shipers are accompanied only by a piano or organ or a single guitar, they are still praising God with the help of other creatures.

I remember times when I have been profoundly moved by music during the Eucharist or other religious services. I think of times when a closing hymn such as "Holy God, We Praise Thy Name" at the end of a festive Mass seemed to lift our hearts right through the roof, and into heaven, so to speak. Even if we were accompanied only by an organ—a complex instrument made up of a variety of "creatures" (wood, metal, ivory, and other materials)—we somehow knew we were praising our Creator in the company of other nonhuman creatures.

Imagine a more complex form of musical accompa-niment—trumpets, violins, French horns, bass fiddles, kettledrums, handbells, and more. We would feel that we are praising God as an even larger family of creatures. In doing this we are being truer to what God ultimately wants us to be—one great family of creation.

Specific Prayers

One of the prayers we frequently hear the priest say at Mass is this:

> Father, you are holy indeed and all
> creation rightly gives you praise.

These are the opening words of Eucharistic Prayer III of the Roman Missal. I love this prayer. The words express clearly and directly our way of including the whole family of creation in our public prayer and liturgical life. We can surely find new ways to apply these words to the creatures we invite to accompany us in praising God here on earth. In fact, when we are blessed someday to enjoy God's loving presence in heaven, we can apply these words to all the creatures praising God with us in that heavenly kingdom.

There is a principle in Catholic theology that goes like this in Latin: *lex orandi, lex credendi.* Translated literally, it means, "The law of prayer is the law of belief." An easier-to-understand translation would be:

> The way we pray indicates
> the way we believe.

To better understand this principle, let us consider Eucharistic Prayer IV that we find in the Roman Missal. Here is the prayer:

> Father, in your mercy grant also to us, your children,
>> to enter into our heavenly inheritance
>> in the company of the Virgin Mary,
>> the Mother of God,
>> and your Apostles and Saints.
> Then, in your kingdom, freed from the corruption of
> sin and death
>> *we shall sing your glory with every creature*
>> through Christ our Lord. . . . (emphasis added)

These words say very clearly (and I quote), that in the next life, "we shall sing your glory with every creature." The words indicate what we believe. As you can see, this is a good example and a reasonable application of the formula: "The way we pray indicates the way we believe."

The words of Eucharist Prayer IV also seem very much in keeping with the spirit of Psalm 148 (as we discussed in chapter 3) and with Psalm 150 (quoted above), not to mention St. Francis's *Canticle of the Creatures*. In each of these hymns of praise, we see all creatures, both human and nonhuman, praising God as one family of creation.

Christians of Many Backgrounds

I have shared with you some of the prayers coming from my Catholic tradition that have taught me how to love and understand other creatures. Now let us look at some of the rich resources that come from other traditions. For example, just as in the last chapter I mentioned a terrific animal blessings service at a Catholic church in San Francisco, let me now tell you how I deepened my understanding while visiting another great animal blessing in an Episcopal church in New York City.

All animal blessings are occasions when people literally pray together with animals and other earthly creatures. I see no way that the annual St. Francis day celebration at the Episcopal Cathedral of St. John the Divine in New York City, the largest Gothic cathedral in the world, can be surpassed in terms of paying honor to God's animal creatures.

The liturgists at St. John's pulled out more stops in their St. Francis Day celebration than I can ever recall experiencing in a Roman Catholic celebration. I was there on Sunday, October 6, 2002, and it was one of the most spectacular animal blessings and celebrations of St. Francis of Assisi that I, a lifelong follower of the saint, had ever seen. Few churches honor the patron saint of ecology with more color and pomp, and with more animals in the pews and aisles, than this great cathedral, located in Upper Manhattan.

I had been aware of this well-known celebration that always takes place on the first Sunday of October in close proximity to the saint's feast day (October 4). I was covering the event in order to prepare a photo story for *St. Anthony Messenger.* But the excitement of being part of this vast, jubilant assembly of people and pets will always remain vibrant in my memory.

For several glorious hours, the immense cathedral, over 600 feet in length, seemed to be transformed into the lost Garden of Paradise. At least, that's how it seemed to me. A standing-room-only crowd of over 3,500 men, women, and children—with dogs, cats, gerbils, turtles, parrots, and other pets at their sides—worshiped and praised their loving Creator with song and dance and colorful banners. The Spirit of St. Francis was truly alive in that holy space.

The Eucharist began with the Paul Winter Consort and the St. Francis Day Festival Chorus breaking into an exuberant adaptation of St. Francis's *Canticle of the Creatures.* In this instance, the chorus and the entire congregation praised God not only through Brother Sun, Sister Moon and Stars, but also through Brother Wolf, Sister Whale, and Sister Loon.

The liturgical ministers, cross-bearers, and dancers, amidst clouds of incense and pulsating rhythms, processed joyfully down the middle aisle, as primordial cries of whale, wolf, and loon sounded forth over the public address system.

Despite the exultant music, praise, and intense motion, the animals in the pews were curiously quiet, save for an occasional howl or whimper, and even that seemed to blend harmoniously with the recorded voices of wolves and whales and other sounds of the deep. It struck me that the immense throng of women and men, as well as animals of land, sea, and air, were worshiping God in one symphony of praise. They had become *one family of creation*, which, according to the perspective of St. Francis of Assisi, is precisely what all of us creatures are intended by God to be.

The joy of the moment was echoed in the opening collect, prayed by the Right Rev. Mark S. Sisk, the Episcopal bishop of New York (who revealed to me that he is also a Third Order Franciscan, a member of what is widely known today as the Secular Franciscan Order): "Most high, almighty, and good Lord, grant . . . that after the example of blessed Francis we may, for love of you, delight in all your creatures . . . through Jesus Christ our Lord. . . ."

Then the dean of the Cathedral, the Very Rev. Dr. James Kowalski, urged listeners in his sermon to thank God "for the special insights that St. Francis has entrusted to us" and "to renew our commitment to being good stewards of the gift of creation."

At the end of the Eucharist, the bishop invited all to recite, as the postcommunion prayer, the familiar *Peace Prayer of St. Francis.*

No sooner, however, did the festive, two-hour celebration of the Eucharist come to an end than the great bronze doors of the cathedral swung open to begin the Blessing of Animals Ceremony. A solemn procession of larger and more exotic animals along with their caretakers began to move down the center aisle in almost complete silence.

Certain details of that day were unforgettable. A man with a huge eagle perched on his gloved hand led the way. The eagle was followed by a large camel, two llamas, a ram, a full-grown bull, a man carrying a boa constrictor, and a woman holding a big blue-gold macaw, to mention a few. The procession of animals finally stopped at the main altar to receive Bishop Sisk's blessing. "Live without fear," the bishop announced gently. "Your Creator loves you, made you holy, and has always protected you. Go in peace to follow the good road, and may God's blessing be with you always.

Amen." It would be difficult to find any way to express this idea better than that.

Once the ceremonies inside the cathedral came to an end, the celebration moved outside onto the spacious lawn alongside the cathedral. A festive fair with various exhibits in place was already being checked out by visitors. The people, holding their small pets or leading dogs by the leash, began forming lines at various venues before members of the clergy on the tree-studded cathedral lawn, to have their animal companions blessed individually. A happy mood prevailed everywhere as it is also a blessing for us to bless our beloved animals. When the wonderful ceremonies of that day came to an end, it was very appropriate that everyone was in a garden of trees and sun-splashed greenery.

I talked with the Dr. Kowalski after the service had ended. "Many people commented about how quiet the cathedral is during a long service like this, with 3,500 people and hundreds of cats, dogs, birds, and other animals," he said. "The harmony and peacefulness in the cathedral touch people deeply. It's a kind of foretaste of the lion and the lamb lying down together. . . . I think St. Francis Day at St. John the Divine is another glimpse of how life is meant to be, with all God's creation not just surviving, but also living interdependently and harmoniously together." Yes, indeed.

He concluded, "Anglicans have developed a creation theology. Anglican divines wrote poetry in which even pebbles of sand on the beach sing out the praises of the Lord. Francis seems to offer us particular hope [insofar as he] identified with the weak, the suffering, and all creatures—great and small. It would be sad to sentimentalize Francis, instead of seeing that *one major healing* is needed on this planet, our fragile island home. What needs healing most urgently is our relationship to creation."

I could not stop thinking about another garden as I caught glimpses of happy clusters of humans enjoying the wonders of nature alongside their blessed animals. For these shining moments we had returned to the Garden of Eden as one family of creation—all aglow with the goodness of God.

Jesus' Resurrection and Ours

8

Our Christian belief in the resurrection of the body can lead us a step closer to the vision of the whole family of creation being included in God's saving plan. The resurrection emphasizes the great significance of our earthly bodies and our earthly environment. At death, our bodies are not discarded like empty shells, as if only our souls are precious and meant to live with God. Not at all! The resurrection affirms that our bodies, too, are precious and destined to rise again like Christ's own body.

In the Gospels, the resurrection stories of Jesus carefully point out that even though Jesus' risen body has
been transformed so that he can pass through closed
doors, his body was not discarded after his death nor did
he lose that part of his human nature. Indeed, in his risen
life he retains his earthly humanity as well as his divinity.
In Luke's Gospel, Jesus tells his disciples, "Look at my
hands and my feet. See that it is I myself. Touch me and
see; for a ghost does not have flesh and bones as you can
see I have" (Luke 24:39, NRSV). Later Jesus said to them,
"Have you anything here to eat?" and in response the
disciples "gave him a piece of broiled fish, and he took
and ate in their presence" (Luke 24:41–43, NRSV).

These stories clearly teach us not only that has Jesus
risen bodily from the dead, but also that those who
believe in him will rise bodily, just as he did.

The following ritual at Catholic funerals supports
the same beliefs. The presiding priest, without uttering
a word, walks slowly and solemnly around the casket,
gently swinging the censor, allowing clouds of fragrant
incense to rise upward to honor the bodily remains of the
person who has died. We aren't simply remembering a
body that has experienced death; we are honoring a body
that will live again as God has promised. This awesome
ritual of respect toward the human body reinforces our

fervent belief that these, our earthly bodies, and all that they represent, are meant to be transformed and saved, as was Jesus' glorified body.

Still, we are keenly aware that our bodies are fragile and are vitally interconnected with the whole created world. Think about it. Our bodies, along with all living creatures, would not survive one minute if the sun suddenly disappeared. If we cut ourselves off from Brother Sun, Brother Air, Sister Water, and Mother Earth, we would by the same stroke cut ourselves off from our source of life because of the intimate linkage between our bodies and our environment.

The doctrine of the resurrection of the body suggests that no genuine part of our human or earthly experience need be lost. I was recently in the chapel of a Catholic retirement home in Cincinnati and was fascinated by the image of Christ hanging behind the altar. In most Catholic churches, one typically sees behind the altar some form of the crucifix; this image, however, was of the risen Christ—or perhaps the risen Christ ascending to the right hand of the Father. The image of our risen Savior struck me as very appropriate for a Christian retirement home. Residents will find comfort, as well as assurance of their own resurrection, as they contemplate the image of the risen Christ as a model for their own resurrection. Old or broken bodies will become new and perfect.

The image prompted me to think again of the painting of the risen and glorified Christ done by Sister Mary Thomas (discussed in chapter 5). In my imagination, I put a copy of her painting over this image of Christ rising bodily to glory. I imagined, too, the multitude of animals, plants, and other creatures, which in her painting become part of the risen Christ. As St. Paul tells us, the glorified Christ is the Lord of all creation, and he holds first place and headship among all creatures. In Paul's own words, "all things were created through him and for him. He is before all things, and in him all things hold together" (Colossians 1:16–17).

In Catholic teaching and practice, the Christ who holds first place among all creatures is described as "Christ the King," and each year our liturgical calendar ends in late November with the feast of "Our Lord Jesus Christ the King." We believe that God gave him headship (primacy, lordship) over all creatures. You and I also believe that we share in his bodily resurrection and glory.

In the course of this book, moreover, I have set forth reasons (from Scripture, from church tradition, from the life of St. Francis, and so forth) that other creatures may well be saved in the "new heavens and new earth" that Scripture talks about and that we will discuss more in the next chapter. It is good for us to hold on to the image of the risen Christ, as portrayed in the painting of Sister Mary Thomas, where all our fellow-creatures are somehow bound up in the resurrection of Christ. Now we might ask: if our human bodies are destined for resurrection with Christ, what does that mean about the bodies of our blessed animal companions?

This may also be a good time to ask again the title question:

"Will I See My Dog in Heaven?"

I have been so focused on the larger question posed by this book—*Will we see the whole family of creation in heaven?*—that I may seem to have ignored the first question. Often that first question—will I see my dog (my cat, my rabbit, my gerbil, my parrot, my turtle) in heaven?—is the question closest to our hearts. The question of the future of our beloved pets holds deep emotional importance for us—and it should.

Although I do not have a dog or a pet at this point in my life, I have some experience of caring for animals and feeling emotional ties to them. Let me tell you a story that takes me back many years. Around 1943, when I was about eight years old, our family had a dog named Toppy, and my older brother, Paul, and I had the responsibility of taking care of him. Toppy, who was part Beagle, was under our care only for a year or two, because it wasn't long before the poor creature got hit and killed by a car. My brother, who witnessed the tragic event, ran into our house, crying inconsolably, and told us the terrible news. I keenly felt that loss, too. Most of my other memories of Toppy, however, have faded by now—after all, it was sixty-five years ago. Yet, for weeks and maybe months after his death, I kept expecting to see Toppy come bounding into our backyard where his doghouse had stood—but Toppy never showed up. Obviously, that strong memory, still vividly with me so many years later, is a clear indication of my own grief. So I understand how difficult it is to lose such a loved one.

Let me tell you a more recent story, as well. Magic is a different dog and a different story altogether. Magic came into my life more recently. Her home is in Seattle, Washington, with my sister and brother-in-law, Tese and Bill Neighbor, and their two teenage boys, Josh and Noah. Magic is a Golden Retriever and still very much alive. I knew Magic as a pup, and my fondness for her is renewed often, thanks to visits with the family in Seattle at Christmastime, and sometimes in the summer as well.

About eight years ago the Neighbors invited me to use their cabin while I was working on a writing project.

Their cabin is located on the Olympic Peninsula, two or three hours west of Seattle. Tese persuaded me that during my two- or three-week stay at the cabin I might want to babysit for Magic, who was just a pup at the time. Her request had its perks. The cabin with its ample deck sits on a wooded hillside and has a panoramic view of the Hood Canal, part of the intercoastal water system that spreads out from Seattle. The area is rich in natural beauty and wildlife. Two bald eagles often perch atop a tall pine tree that towers over the cabin. Those awesome birds seem to have come with the property.

To breathe in all this beauty and bond with this affectionate pup were great blessings for me. Besides feeding and watching over Magic, I took breaks from my writing project and went on happy walks with her on scenic forest paths along the canal.

As time went on, Magic began living up to her name as a *retriever*. Three or four years later she displayed incredible retrieving skills at the cabin. Somehow Magic had learned to retrieve bright green tennis balls thrown off the cabin deck toward the canal that spreads out like a huge lake down below. The cabin's deck must be sixty feet above the surface of the water. To get to the water, Magic had to race down fifteen or so wooden steps connecting the deck to the ground below, then charge some twenty yards down the steep hillside through the shrubs and undergrowth, down twenty more wooden steps to the level of the canal—and finally dash another few yards to reach the water. During one of my summer visits about a decade ago, Magic came to me with a tennis ball clenched in her teeth and dropped it at my feet on the deck, then looked up at me with her bright eyes, as if to say, "Try me out!"

Having played baseball as a teenager, I still had a fairly good arm. After warming up a bit, I threw the ball over the top branches of a row of tall evergreens that partially blocked the view of the canal from spectators on the deck, including Magic. Magic watched my wind-up and throw quite carefully. Then after catching only a split-second glimpse of the ball's trajectory, she charged down the steps and hillside and soon plunged into the water below. Amazingly, within two or three minutes she came rushing back onto the deck and dropped the ball at my feet. She looked up at me again with her bright eyes and playful grin. *This girl really loves being a retriever*, I thought with amazement. And as I soon found out, Magic could keep playing this game for hours.

I know that some people say animals don't have souls. I have no problem agreeing that they don't have exactly the same kind of souls that humans have. But I have a hard time accepting that an animal like Magic does not have a soul, great intelligence, and an amazing set of instincts. Nobody can say that she does not have a mighty heart, a wonderful sense of play, and a great capacity to give and receive affection. I hope most people will at least agree that she has received amazing gifts from our Creator.

Happily, another very appealing dog has come into my life within the last year or so—a little white Shih Tzu named Tita. She's as cute as a button and is often a guest at Pleasant Street Friary in Cincinnati's inner city, where I live with five other Franciscan friars. Tita belongs to a friend of Mark, one of the friars with whom I live, and is with us one or two days a week, or even more when her owner is called out of town. She is a hit with everyone because she brings her own brand of joy and affection into the friary.

Jim, one of the other friars, has taught her a few tricks such as rolling over, extending her paw for a "hand-shake," and standing on her hind legs to ask for a bit of food. Tita sometimes joins us when our small community of friars gathers for the Eucharist. She is always very quiet and reverent during Mass, and some of us enjoy greeting Tita at the "sign of peace." We are happy to have this wonderful fellow creature "praising God" with us at times in our friary. In her own mysterious and "doggy" way, Tita is a little mirror of the goodness and love of God that we celebrate in the Eucharist.

Then there is one more dog that I feel compelled to tell you about, because she brought great peace to my soul three or four years ago. I was visiting some good friends who introduced me to their dog, Pippy, a full-grown, chocolate Labrador Retriever. I was seated when they brought the dog into the room. A rather large dog, he came up close and sat upright directly in front of me. He just sat there in silence, hardly a foot away from my face, looking into my eyes with an expression of gentle sadness. He did this more than once during my visit.

Quite puzzled by what was going on between Pippy and me, I asked Pippy's owners what they thought was happening. My friends, who knew that my mother had died from cancer two or three weeks earlier, told me that Pippy had probably sensed my emotional pain and felt a sympathetic connection with me. That rang true, because my heart had been deeply wrenched by my mother's death, and I could feel a real flow of compassion coming from Pippy. It's a very comforting memory for me. Pippy just sat there and kept looking at me in silence as if saying, "I feel your loss."

I've also had opportunities in recent years to house-sit for families who have cats. I enjoy watching these beautiful creatures, too, even though they are usually quite reserved and reluctant to show feelings. Like many kids who grew up in a small rural town, I have good memories of caring for other critters like frogs, turtles, rabbits, and baby chicks.

In this book I have set forth reasons suggesting that creatures other than humans will find a place in that "new heaven and new earth" that the Bible talks about and that we will discuss more in the next chapter. In the creation accounts of Genesis, we have learned that all creatures are good and reflect the goodness of God. It is easy for me to recognize this same goodness not only in the abstract, but also when I think specifically of Toppy, Magic, Tita, Pippy, and other creatures I've come to know.

In a similar vein, I have discussed in previous chapters the belief that God, having entering our created world through the Incarnation, elevated the dignity not only of humans but also of animals. Again I find it meaningful to apply this elevated dignity to Magic and Tita and to all of our animal companions. The same is true of the principal of sacramentality—the belief that every created thing can be a sign or "sacrament" of the divine. This can certainly apply to all of our pets.

If I can accept St. Paul's teaching in Colossians that somehow all creatures are present in Christ, the glorified Lord of all creation, I can see our pets included in is way of thinking also. The Irish poet Joseph Mary Plunkett

(1887–1916) seems to have expressed this same outlook in his poem "I See His Blood upon the Rose." Plunkett's vision in this poem is very similar to the vision of St. Paul, namely, that the risen and glorified Christ is somehow intertwined with the whole family of creation.

Before looking at the poem, you may find these awesome facts about the author's last days interesting. An Irish nationalist, Plunkett took part in the Easter Rising of 1916 to win independence from Britain. He was imprisoned in Dublin by the English army. Just hours before his execution by a firing squad on May 14, he married his fiancée, Grace Clifford, in the jail's chapel. He was only twenty-eight years old.

"I See His Blood upon the Rose" suggests to me that Joseph Plunkett envisioned Christ's destiny and great love as forever entwined with this earth and this universe:

> I see his blood upon the rose
> And in the stars the glory of his eyes,
> His body gleams amid eternal snows,
> His tears fall from the skies.
>
> I see his face in every flower;
> The thunder and the singing of the birds
> Are but his voice—and carven by his power
> Rocks are his written words.

All pathways by his feet are worn,

His strong heart stirs the ever-beating sea,

His crown of thorns is twined with every thorn,

His cross is every tree.[15]

Bodily Resurrection?

So, then, what about the resurrection of our own bodies and the bodies of our beloved animals? I would like to answer this question by sharing with you a quote from St. Paul's letter to the Philippians that very recently caught me by surprise: "Our citizenship is in heaven, and from it we also await a savior, the Lord Jesus Christ. He will change our lowly body to conform with his glorified body by the power that enables him also to bring all things into subjection to himself" (Philippians 3:20–21).

These words caught me by surprise because they shed amazing light on various points expressed in this chapter. Paul is assuring us that our true home ("our citizenship") is in heaven. He assures us further that our bodies too are destined to rise again and be transformed like Christ's own body. Paul also tells us that Christ, as the Lord of Creation, is able "to bring all things into subjection to himself." He is saying that our Savior somehow contains "all things" in his risen body, as the painting of Sister Mary Thomas strongly suggests. Paul thus seems to be saying that "all things"—whether human, animal, plant, or mineral—are somehow meant to be saved and summed up in the risen Christ.

If we believe, therefore, in these words of St. Paul and in our wider Judeo-Christian vision, I feel we can make a good case for saying, "Yes, in some mysterious but real way, our animal, plant, and mineral companions, or 'brothers' and 'sisters,' will be with us in the restored Garden of Eden."

9

Images from
the Book of Revelation

In chapter 5 of the book of Revelation,
the inspired writer John gives us an intriguing
description of a vision he saw when he was a prisoner on
the Greek island of Patmos. The vision is reminiscent of
Psalm 148 (see chapter 3), because it gives us a glimpse
of all creatures of the universe praising God together.

In his vision, John sees God sitting on a glorious throne in heaven. Standing near the throne is Jesus in the form of a lamb. An immense crowd of angels and human beings are also there before God and the Lamb. Here is John's testimony:

> Then I heard every creature in heaven and on earth and under the earth and in the sea, everything in the universe cry out: "To the one who sits on the throne and to the Lamb be blessing and honor, glory and might, forever and ever." (Revelation 5:13)

What we see here, in the last book of the Bible, is the whole family of creation praising God and the Lamb. We know that the book of Revelation often communicates its message symbolically rather than literally. Whatever way we look at John's vision, however, he seems to be affirming that all creatures of the universe are in the presence of God, and blessing him with "honor and glory . . . forever and ever."

There are many other visions in the book of Revelation. A very significant one appears early in chapter one. John describes for "the seven churches in Asia" and for all who read this book a powerful vision he had of "Jesus Christ

. . . the firstborn of the dead and ruler of the kings of the earth" (Revelation 1:5a). While on Patmos, John heard behind him "a voice as loud as a trumpet. . . . Then I turned to see whose voice it was that spoke to me," he writes, "and when I turned, I saw seven gold lampstands and in the midst of the lampstands one like the son of man, wearing an ankle-length robe, with a gold sash around his chest. The hair of his head was white as white wool or as snow, and his eyes were like a fiery flame . . . and his face shone like the sun at its brightest.

"When I caught sight of him, I fell to the ground as though dead. He touched me with his right hand and said, 'Do not be afraid. I am the first and the last, the one who lives. Once I was dead, but now I am alive forever and ever'" (Revelation 1:10–14, 16–18a). John's vision here, of course, is a description of the risen and glorified Christ—the Christ who has triumphed over death and remains faithful to those faithful to him.

Near the end of Revelation, John has another vision of special importance: "Then I saw a new heaven and a new earth. The former heaven and the former earth had passed away, and the sea was no more" (Revelation 21:1). This image of "a new heaven and a new earth" reminds us of the original Garden of Paradise before the fall, when everything was in harmony—when Adam

and Eve and other creatures lived innocently and peacefully with each other in God's presence. He seems to be
showing us the future of what is to come.

The book of Revelation wants to make clear that just
as there was a freshly created garden in the first book of
the Bible, so there is a second garden in the final book
of the Bible. John sees this second garden in Revelation
21, describing it as "a new heaven and a new earth."
Biblical scholar Luke Timothy Johnson points out: "As
Genesis began with creation by a word, so the vision of
the end-time [in the book of Revelation] recapitulates
that beginning: creation is renewed." [16]

It's clear that the inspired author of Revelation bor-
rowed this image from the prophet Isaiah, who writes
the following bold, hope-filled message: "Lo, I am about
to create new heavens and a new earth; The things of
the past [that is, the long period of time during which
the original harmony was absent] shall not be remem-
bered or come to mind. . . . No longer shall the sound
of weeping be heard there, or the sound of crying; No
longer shall there be in it an infant who lives but a few
days, or an old man who does not round out his full
lifetime. . . . The wolf and the lamb shall graze alike,
and the lion shall eat hay like an ox" (Isaiah 65:17,
19–20a, 25a).

What Isaiah is showing us here is his vision of a future era in which the original state of peace and harmony in the Garden of Eden, lost through disobedience and sin, is restored. In this new world, there will be no pain or sorrow or enmity or untimely death, only happiness and rejoicing. Even the animals will return to a state of innocence and bliss.

We should also consider an earlier passage from the book of Isaiah (11:1–9) that looks forward to the future Messiah and to the new age of peace he is to usher in. The passage is similar to the one just quoted: "[A] shoot shall sprout from the stump of Jesse [the father of King David], and from his roots a bud shall blossom. The spirit of the LORD shall rest upon him. . . . he shall judge the poor with justice, and decide aright for the land's afflicted. . . . Then the wolf shall be a guest of the lamb, and the leopard shall lie down with the kid; The calf and the young lion shall browse together, with a little child to guide them."

The Catholic Study Bible sums up the above passages from Isaiah with these words found in a footnote: "This picture of the idyllic harmony of paradise is a dramatic symbol of the universal peace and justice of the messianic times."[17]

Clearly, the author of Revelation goes out of his way to show that, just as the first book of the Bible began with an ideal Garden Paradise where God, humans, and beasts dwelt peacefully together, so now the Bible's final book ends with the original garden of harmony and peace restored.

We see in the pages of this final book familiar images from the original Garden: rivers of life and the tree of life. "A river rises in Eden to water the garden," we read in Genesis 2:10. The river soon divides into four rivers, and, as we already know from an earlier verse, "the tree of life [stands] in the middle of the Garden" (see Genesis 2:9). Both the rivers and the tree of life are clear symbols of life and nourishment provided by the Creator. When we come to the new heavens and the new earth in the book of Revelation, these same symbols reveal even richer sources of divine goodness, nourishment, and healing.

The most wonderful expression of this is at the beginning of chapter 22 of the book of Revelation, where, as usual, John is the speaker: "Then the angel showed me the river of life-giving water, sparkling like crystal, flowing from the throne of God and of the Lamb down the middle of its street [of the holy city, the new Jerusalem]. On either side of the river grew the tree of life that produces fruit twelve times a year, once each month; the leaves of the trees serve as medicine for the nations" (Revelation 22:1–2).

We can rather easily grasp the symbolism. We will be in the restored Garden of Eden. The river of life and the tree of life are there. The river of life, moreover, is flowing from the throne of God (the Father) and of the Lamb (now glorified and with the Father). As biblical scholars point out, the river of life is a symbol of the Holy Spirit, and thus we have an allusion to the Trinity as well.

The scene is also a picture of super fertility and abundance: the sparkling stream flowing from the throne has become a river. Now there are two trees of life, rather than one, and they have twelve harvests a year rather than one. And the leaves of the trees have a healing effect on the nations. The fertility and abundance of this garden is unmistakable. It is quite obvious that the author of Revelation drew his image of the wonderful stream of water and its abundant harvest from chapter 47 of Ezekiel.

Our focus is on the river and on the tree of life, because they are key symbols of the original Paradise in which God, humans, and other creatures lived in harmony. This, in turn, is a symbol of what we may expect in heaven.

There are several other places in the book of Revelation where the image of the tree of life is mentioned. One is where John writes to the "seven churches in Asia" (Revelation 1:4). In his letter to the Church of Ephesus,

John, speaking for the Spirit, writes: "To the victor I will give the right to eat from the tree of life that is in the garden of God" (Revelation 2:7b). *The Catholic Study Bible* explains, again in a footnote, that *victor* refers "to any Christian individual who holds fast to the faith and does God's will in the face of persecution. The tree of life that is in the garden of God [refers] to the tree in the primeval paradise" (Genesis 2:9). The footnote states further: "The decree excluding humanity from the tree of life has been revoked by Christ."[18]

I should add that over the centuries many Christian saints and scholars have pointed out that the tree of life is a symbol of both Christ and the cross of Christ, through whom we gain the fullness of life. The Franciscan theologian and writer St. Bonaventure, for example, wrote a thirteenth-century mystical treatise entitled *The Tree of Life*, in which he identifies this symbol with both Christ and his cross.

All of these hopeful Scripture passages about a future paradise, the state of happiness we commonly call heaven, brings my thoughts back to Pippy, mentioned in the last chapter. Thanks to his compassionate gaze into my eyes, Pippy helped remove some of the pain I was carrying in my heart caused by my mother's death. Pippy connected with me in a profound way that wasn't human, but was creature to creature.

In the new heavens and the new earth, described by Isaiah, the lion and the lamb and many other creatures live together in happy harmony. One of the themes of this book is that the whole family of creation is meant to walk together in peace and harmony on this earth as they journey to God. I found Pippy helpful to me in my own life's journey, in that he made my mother's death easier to bear. Of course, many loving human beings also consoled me in similar ways through their prayers, words, and loving support. Yet, it is, indeed, consoling to remember that our animal companions are also able to support us in such stressful situations.

This also applies to a host of other sister and brother creatures. Consider, for example, how Brother Sun and Sister Water can cheer and heal our troubled hearts as we walk along an ocean beach, a lake, or a river. Or how our sisters the birds or our brothers the trees and flowering bushes remind us of God's care as we stroll through a park or forest. I believe, moreover, that our Creator wants the peace or consolation that we experience in such settings to be a foretaste of the final paradise to come.

The New Jerusalem

There is another image from Revelation that follows immediately after John's vision of "a new heaven and a new earth," and that is the "new Jerusalem."

John writes: "I also saw the holy city, the new Jerusalem, coming down out of heaven from God, prepared as a bride adorned for her husband. I heard a loud voice from the throne saying, 'Behold, God's dwelling is with the human race. He will dwell with them and they will be his people and God himself will always be with them (as their God)'" (Revelation 21:2–3). This idea, too, has implications for our hope that we will see our pets and other creatures in heaven.

The idea expresses an amazingly intense and loving, marriagelike union between God and his people. This intimate union would be a state of happiness not unlike heaven itself. In fact, if we were to die in that kind of union with God, we would indeed be in heaven. Even now, if we are trying to live our lives out of love for God and according to God's plan, we would be enjoying a heavenlike state, would we not?—or at least a *foretaste* of the heaven still to come?

After announcing, through John, this kind of union between God and the human race, and God's dwelling with us as our God, "The one who sat on the throne said, 'Behold, I make all things new'" (Revelation 21:5). I find this statement "I make all things new" very curious. God seems to be going well beyond making *all human beings* new to say "I make *all things* new." *All things* is the literal translation of the Greek word *panta*. The word is clearly neuter and would refer to all things of creation taken together, including human, animal, plant, and mineral.

If we look at the translation of this idea ("Behold, I make all things new") in *The Jerusalem Bible*, it strikes us as being even more dramatic. *The Jerusalem Bible* translation is: "Now I am making the whole of creation new." This would certainly be a valid translation of *panta*.

We are getting back to a theme we have discovered often in the Bible—that God's saving love includes the whole family of creation, not only the human beings.

God's creating "a new heaven and a new earth" is much broader and drastic than simply initiating a new love relationship with human beings—as beautiful and sublime as that idea is. As we come to the closing pages of this book, you and I must admit once again that our knowledge is finite and limited. We really do not have a full idea of the extent of God's wonderful plans for those who love him; "What no eye has seen, nor ear heard, nor the human heart conceived, what God has prepared for those who love him. . . ." (1 Corinthians 2:9, NRSV). We have good reason to believe, moreover, from the passages of Scripture we have been examining, that ultimately we will somehow find the whole family of creation, including our beloved animals, in that "new heaven and new earth" seen by St. John.

Jesus once said that we are to have faith like children. Sometimes I find that children can see and understand those things that we adults, for whatever reasons, no longer seem to see or understand quite as clearly. Support for our hope in matters of faith often comes from unexpected sources. Many people whose pets have died, for example, have personally told me that they just "know" in their hearts or by some inner intuition that their beloved dog or cat or parrot is in heaven. I also believe that little children may have a similar instinct or inner sense about their pets and other animals being in heaven.

Jesus once uttered this prayer: "I bless you, Father, Lord of heaven and of earth, for hiding these things from the learned and the clever and revealing them to mere children" (Matthew 11:25, JB). In this spirit, I have something similar to share with you: thanks to the kind assistance of a friend, an elementary school teacher in Cincinnati, eight first-grade students offered these brief answers to my question:

"Why Should Animals Go to Heaven?"

1. "If they didn't go to heaven, who would take care of them?" (Jackson)
2. "So they can be with their owner who loves them." (Liz)
3. "Because it's the only place for them to go if they are good." (Jakari)
4. "Because they are good." (Nathan)
5. "Because God loves his creations." (Leah)
6. "Because he [God] loves them and wants them to live with him." (Amber)
7. "When it dies, where else would it go?" (Rachel)
8. "If only *people* were in heaven, it would be boring." (Radu)

We may not know exactly how God will bring the whole family of creation some day to heaven. What we do know is this: our faith, supported by Scripture, Christian teaching, and the life of St. Francis, gives us solid hints and clues that if we live in harmony with God's plans, we will see the "whole of creation" in heaven.

Creation Yearning to Be Free

10.

In this final chapter, I will summarize all that I have been trying to say in *Will I See My Dog in Heaven?* I also hope to show that all creation is, indeed, yearning to be free. In either case, my concluding thoughts begin appropriately with the death of St. Francis.

When Francis of Assisi's days on earth were growing short, according to his first biographer, Thomas of Celano, he made this request of his brothers: "When you see that I am brought to my last moments, place me naked upon the ground . . . and let me lie there after I am dead for the length of time it takes to walk one mile unhurriedly."[19]

After Francis died, his brothers honored his wishes: They placed his body upon Mother Earth, where it lay for some thirty minutes.

What an unusual gesture for a saint. Is this what you would normally associate with holiness—lying down on the ground to symbolize your close relationship to the earth? Probably not, and neither would I. But Francis showed us something different. This gesture of Francis's and of his friars seems to reveal how comfortable and familiar Francis had become with our created world, and how much he valued it as an essential connection to his own life. Like Adam before the Fall, Francis, in his innocence, was not ashamed of his nakedness. Francis had become deeply aware that Jesus, through the Incarnation, had touched and transformed the earth and the human form. The saint came to believe that both of these, the earth and his body, were profoundly good.

Shortly before he died, Francis also "invited all creatures to praise God, and by means of the words he had composed earlier [in the *Canticle of the Creatures*], he exhorted them to love God."[20] It is most telling that Francis, near the moment of his death, was very conscious of including his sister and brother creatures in his final prayer of praise to God.

Francis, moreover, also exhorted death itself—so feared by many—to give praise to God. In fact, "going joyfully to meet [death], [Francis] invited it to make its lodging with him. 'Welcome,' he said, 'my sister death.' "[21]

Some months earlier, he had added these words to his *Canticle of the Creatures*:

All praise be yours, my Lord,
   through Sister bodily death,
From whose embrace no mortal can escape.
How dreadful for those who die in sin.
How lovely for those found in Your Most Holy Will.
   The second death can do them no harm.

As Francis, during his life, had often honored his sister and brother birds with his joyful attention, now these creatures wanted to honor their "brother" as his soul rose to meet the glorified Jesus. Thus, St. Bonaventure ended his *Life of St. Francis* with these poetic words regarding the numerous larks that gathered in the air directly above Francis's hut:

Larks are birds
that love the light and dread the twilight darkness.
But at the hour of the holy man's passing,
although it was twilight and night was to follow,
they came in a great flock
over the roof of the house
and, whirling around for a long time
with unusual joy,
gave clear and evident testimony
of the glory of the saint,
who so often had invited them
to praise God.[22]

After Francis's death, Thomas of Celano writes, "One of Francis's brothers, a man of some renown, saw the soul of the most holy father, like a star . . . ascending over many waters and borne aloft on a little white cloud, going directly to heaven."[23] Through the embrace of Sister Death, Francis was set free from the sorrows of this earthly life and was borne up to meet the risen Christ. As we noted in chapter 8, our Christian doctrine of the resurrection of the body assures us that no genuine part of our human and earthly experience need be lost.

We come back, therefore, to our original question— the question our children ask so earnestly:

Will I see my dog in heaven?

As we've explored, the question may at first seem a bit naïve and simplistic. To many, it will always seem thus. But when we rephrase the question in broader spiritual and theological terms: "Does God intend the *whole* created world somehow to be saved?" it loses some of its naïve overtones.

And from all the evidence, I believe we can make a good case for the hope imbedded in each human heart. Our hope is this: that the whole family of creation will someday share in the fullness of salvation won by Jesus Christ. The more we see the full implications of our belief in the resurrection of the body and accept the biblical vision of God's inclusive love, the easier it is to give a hopeful answer not only to our children's questions, but also to those of us adults.

In the final analysis, how many of us are truly satisfied with a vision of heaven that does not include the whole family of creation? We take comfort, therefore, in St. Paul's words: "We know that the whole creation has been groaning in labor pains until now" for its freedom and redemption (see Romans 8:22, NRSV). Moreover, we embrace the great apostle's hope "that the creation itself will be set free from its bondage to decay and will obtain the freedom of the glory of the children of God" (Romans 8:21, NRSV). Commenting on the word *decay* in this verse, biblical scholar Joseph A. Fitzmyer, SJ, writes that the word refers to "not just moral corruption, but the reign of dissolution and death found in physical creation. Material creation is thus not to be a mere spectator of humanity's triumphant glory and freedom, but to share in it. When the children of God are finally revealed in glory, the material world will also be emancipated from the 'last enemy'" (see 1 Corinthians 15:23–28). When we look at 1 Corinthians 15:26 (NRSV) we discover very precisely that "the last enemy to be destroyed is death."[24]

I have been struggling with these questions all of my life. I realize this struggle now—more than ever—as I write this book while living in my eighth decade. In fact, all of these questions take me back to 1964, when I was a young twenty-seven-year-old Franciscan priest in Louisville, Kentucky, taking a creative writing course at the University of Louisville. I wrote the following poem at that time—a poem that has never strayed far from my awareness in the years that followed:

An Apology for Artists

An old monk made some tiger cubs
  from lumps of moldy clay,
then found a block of cherry wood
  and gaily carved a tray.
His abbot caught him later still
  with water paints and brush,
all smiles, and dabbing speckles
  on a fresh and dazzling thrush.
"Jerome! Jerome!" the abbot cried,
  "explain these vain distractions!
A monk should paint Madonnas—
  depict nice, pious actions."
"Well, tell me sir," the monk replied,
  while brushing off his habit,
"did God give you a good excuse
  for making fox and rabbit?"

Never knowing that my life would become so dedicated
to the questions that we've been pursuing throughout
these chapters, I see now that my simple poem has a direct
bearing on the major themes of this book. I was totally
unaware of this, however, when I wrote the poem.

In a sense the poem is an apology (or defense) of God,
the Creator-Artist, for making "fox and rabbit" as well

as all the other creatures that inhabit this universe. The "old monk" creating "tiger cubs from lumps of moldy clay" is not unlike the Creator of Adam, who formed the "first man" out of the earth's clay. And the image of the old monk, "all smiles, and dabbing speckles on a fresh and dazzling thrush" was deliberately so-described to reflect the goodness and joy of the Artist *par excellence,* making creatures that mirrored his own goodness and graciousness.

Of course, the old monk is also a symbol of me, the would-be poet, a student at a so-called secular university. Understand that I had just completed twenty-one uninterrupted years of Catholic education: eight years of Catholic elementary school followed by some thirteen years in the Franciscan seminary system. Sitting with feelings of insecurity in this creative-writing class, I was asking myself whether I need a "good excuse" for sitting there: what am I, a Franciscan friar, doing in a literature class in a secular university? Despite my insecurities, I am now convinced that this was a vitally important broadening and humanizing experience for me.

I am now asking a similar question in this book: does our most holy and good Creator-God need "a good excuse" from us or our permission before making "profane" creatures like foxes and rabbits, thrushes and larks, trees, rivers, and stars—and before "populating" heaven with them? I believe the drift of my poem is quite obvious: no, God does not need our permission, or a "good excuse," for making fox and rabbit. And as far as the final paradise goes, God does not need his creatures' permission to fill his "new heaven and new earth" with the whole family of creation. Nor did God need *our* permission to place them in that first primeval Paradise.

This gift of life with God in a "new heaven and a new earth" comes simply from God's own overflowing love and goodness. What is more, in this restored garden-still-to-come there will be no wall of separation between the holy and the profane, the sacred and the secular. That wall is one that *we* make, and, of course, it does not exist in the eye of God. In heaven, the holiness of all God's creatures will be apparent. Even though all of us earthly creatures are clearly distinct from God, we will yet, somehow, be one with God and the risen Jesus. "[God] is not far from any of us," as St. Paul reminded the Athenians. "For 'in him we live and move and have our being'" (Acts 17:27b–28a).

In this "new heaven and new earth," God will walk side by side with all of us. At the same time, "the wolf shall be the guest of the lamb" (Isaiah 11:6), and, hopefully, the fox will live with the rabbit, and we humans will be the happy companions and loving caregivers of our dogs and cats—and all the other creatures.

To answer the title question on the cover of this book, I have come to believe that, "Yes, with heartfelt thanks to God's saving love for the whole family of creation, *I will see my dog in heaven!*"

Acknowledgments

During the preparation of this book, I was greatly blessed to have the guidance of two kind Franciscan confreres and Scripture experts.

In the 1960s Father Hilarion Kistner, OFM, was my Scripture professor at St. Leonard College, our Franciscan house of theology near Dayton, Ohio. In those years he was introducing Franciscan theological students at St. Leonard to some of the latest approaches to Scripture-study flowing from the Second Vatican Council. Fr. Hilarion holds a doctorate of Sacred Theology from the Catholic University of America and a licentiate in Sacred Scripture from the Pontifical Biblical Institute in Rome. From 1986 to the present, Fr. Hilarion has been very busy as the resident biblical advisor and theologian at St. Anthony Messenger Press as well as editor of *Sunday Homily Helps*.

While taking sabbatical studies (1993–94) at the Franciscan School of Theology in Berkeley, California, I had the good fortune, as well, to enjoy to the friendship of Father Michael Guinan, OFM. Fr. Michael is a friar of the Santa Barbara, California, Province of Franciscan Friars and has been a nationally known Scripture professor at the Franciscan School of Theology for over twenty-five years. Fr. Michael, who has a PhD from the Catholic University of America, has written several books and prize-winning articles on biblical topics.

I am most grateful to both Fr. Hilarion and Fr. Michael for their kind, personal assistance to me during the writing of *Will I See My Dog in Heaven?* They generously reviewed each of the ten chapters of this book and provided me with helpful feedback, advice, and wise guidance from their respective storehouses of biblical knowledge and Franciscan spirituality.

I also want to acknowledge the help and support of my family, my confreres, relatives, coworkers, and special friends who have read various parts of this manuscript and have made suggestions regarding style and word choice or provided new ideas and insights. In many ways this has been a community project. My thanks go out to one and all.

I owe special acknowledgement, as well, to Lil Copan, Jon Sweeney, Bob Edmonson, and other editors of Paraclete Press for their insightful guidance and help in the development and revision of this book.

Readers may be interested in how I selected the translations for the Scriptures quoted throughout the text: My custom has always been to check at least three translations—New American Bible (NAB), New Revised Standard Version (NRSV), and The Jerusalem Bible (JB)—in choosing the translation that best expresses the point I am making. In this book, you will see references marked with NRSV or JB. The Noah references, the Jonah references, and the Psalm references are taken from the NRSV and are noted. All other unmarked Scriptures are taken from the NAB.

Appendix
Three Prayers of Blessing for Any Animal, Fish, Bird, or Other Creature

Feel free to gather your family and friends together for these blessings—it is good to have as much of the family of God present, as possible.

You are encouraged to insert the name of your animal companion into these prayers.

Scripture Reflection

"[Christ] is before all things, and in him all things hold together." (Colossians 1:17, NRSV)

For Any of God's Creatures

Blessed are you, Lord God,
Maker of all living creatures.
On the fifth and sixth days of creation,
you called forth fish in the sea,
birds in the air, and animals on the land.
You inspired St. Francis to call all animals
his brothers and sisters.
We ask you to bless this animal (these animals)
gathered about us.
By the power of your love,
enable him or her (them) to live according to your plan.
May we always praise you
for all your beauty in creation.
Blessed are you, Lord our God, in all your creatures.
Amen.

For One or More Sick Creatures

Heavenly Creator,
you made all things for your glory
and made us caretakers of this creature
(these creatures) under our care.
Restore to health and strength this animal
(this pet) that you have entrusted to us.
Keep this animal (this pet)
always under your loving protection.
Blessed are you, Lord God,
And holy is your name for ever and ever. Amen.

For an Animal that Has Died or Is About to Die

Loving God,

our beloved pet and companion, (name),

is on its final journey.

We will miss (name) dearly

because of the joy and affection

(name) has given to us.

Bless (name) and give him/her peace.

May your care for (name) never die.

We thank you for the gift

that (name) has been to us.

Give us hope that in your great kindness

you may restore (name) in your heavenly kingdom

according to your wisdom, which goes

beyond our human understanding. Amen.

Notes

1. Sawyer's comment is found in *The Daily Study Bible, Isaiah*, Vol. 1 (Philadelphia: Westminster Press, 1984), 122.

2. Ilia Delio, Keith Douglass Warner, and Pamela Wood, *Care for Creation: A Franciscan Spirituality of the Earth* (Cincinnati: St. Anthony Messenger Press, 2008), 75, 77, 79.

3. All quotations from both stories are from the NRSV.

4. Marion A. Habig, OFM, ed., *St. Francis of Assisi: Writings and Early Biographies, English Omnibus of Sources for the Life of St. Francis*, Vol. I, Celano XXIX, 80 (Cincinnati, St. Anthony Messenger Press, 2008), 296.

5. See *Francis of Assisi, the Saint: Early Documents*, Vol. 1, 124. Regis J. Armstrong, OFM CAP; J.A. Wayne Hellmann, OFM CONV; William J. Short, OFM, eds. (New York: New York City Press 1999).

6. *The Canticle of Brother Sun,* in Habig, ed., *St. Francis of Assisi*, Vol. 1, Celano, 130–31.

7. Habig, ed., *St. Francis of Assisi*, Vol. 1, *Writings of St. Francis*, V, 139.

8. See the full text at www.usccb.org.

9. St. Bonaventure, *Life of St. Francis*, XII, 2, Classics of Western Spirituality (Mahwah, NJ: Paulist Press, 1978), 294.

10. St. Bonaventure, *The Life of St. Francis*, 294–95.

11. Habig, ed., *St. Francis of Assisi*, Vol. I, Celano XXI, 1:58, 278.

12. Pierre Teilhard de Chardin, *Science and Christ*, as quoted by *St. Anthony Messenger*, November 1993, p. 22.

13. Father Stephen Doyle, OFM, *Ephesians and Colossians*, Cassette 118 (Cincinnati, OH: St. Anthony Messenger Press Audiotape Cassette).

14. *San Francisco Examiner*, October 6, 1996.

15. *The Poems of Joseph Mary Plunkett* (Dublin, Ireland: Talbot Press, 1917), 50.

16. *The Catholic Study Bible* (Oxford, UK: Oxford University Press, 1990), 576 (Reading Guide).

17. *The Catholic Study Bible*, 891.

18. *The Catholic Study Bible*, 891.

19. Habig, ed., *St. Francis of Assisi*, Vol. 1, Celano CLXIII, 217, 536.

20. Habig, ed., *St. Francis of Assisi*, Vol. 1, Celano CLXIII, 217, 536.

21. Habig, ed., *St. Francis of Assisi*, Vol. 1, Celano CLXIII, 217, 536.

22. St. Bonaventure, *The Life of St. Francis*, 320.

23. Habig, ed., *St. Francis of Assisi*, Vol. 1, Celano CLXIII, 217a, 537.

24. Joseph A. Fitzmyer, *The New Jerome Biblical Commentary: The Letter to the Romans* (Englewood Cliffs, NJ: Prentice Hall, 1990), #87, 21, p. 854.

About Paraclete Press

Who We Are

Paraclete Press is a publisher of books, recordings, and DVDs on Christian spirituality. Our publishing represents a full expression of Christian belief and practice—from Catholic to Evangelical, from Protestant to Orthodox.

We are the publishing arm of the Community of Jesus, an ecumenical monastic community in the Benedictine tradition. As such, we are uniquely positioned in the marketplace without connection to a large corporation and with informal relationships to many branches and denominations of faith.

What We Are Doing

Books | Paraclete publishes books that show the richness and depth of what it means to be Christian. Although Benedictine spirituality is at the heart of all that we do, we publish books that reflect the Christian experience across many cultures, time periods, and houses of worship. We publish books that nourish the vibrant life of the church and its people—books about spiritual practice, formation, history, ideas, and customs.

We have several different series, including the best-selling Living Library, Paraclete Essentials, and Paraclete

Giants series of classic texts in contemporary English; A Voice from the Monastery—men and women monastics writing about living a spiritual life today; award-winning literary faith fiction and poetry; and the Active Prayer Series that brings creativity and liveliness to any life of prayer.

Recordings | From Gregorian chant to contemporary American choral works, our music recordings celebrate sacred choral music through the centuries. Paraclete distributes the recordings of the internationally acclaimed choir Gloriæ Dei Cantores, praised for their "rapt and fathomless spiritual intensity" by *American Record Guide,* and the Gloriæ Dei Cantores Schola, which specializes in the study and performance of Gregorian chant. Paraclete is also the exclusive North American distributor of the recordings of the Monastic Choir of St. Peter's Abbey in Solesmes, France, long considered to be a leading authority on Gregorian chant.

DVDs | Our DVDs offer spiritual help, healing, and biblical guidance for life issues: grief and loss, marriage, forgiveness, anger management, facing death, and spiritual formation.

Learn more about us at our Web site:
www.paracletepress.com • 1-800-451-5006.

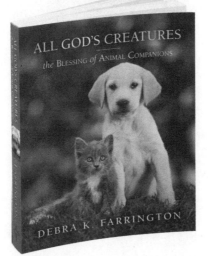

You may also be interested in...

The St. Francis Prayer Book:
A Guide to Deepen Your Spiritual Life

Jon M. Sweeney

ISBN: 978-1-55725-352-1; Paperback $14.95

This warm-hearted little book is a window into the soul of St. Francis, one of the most passionate and inspiring followers of Jesus. With this guide, readers will:

—Pray the words that Francis taught his spiritual brothers and sisters to pray.
—Explore Francis's time and surroundings and feel the joy and earnestness of the first Franciscans.
—Experience how it is possible to live a contemplative and active life, at the same time.

Praise for Aravind Adiga's

LAST MAN IN TOWER

"A rare achievement. . . . Adiga captures with heartbreaking authenticity the real struggle in Indian cities, which is for dignity. A funny yet deeply melancholic work, *Last Man in Tower* is a brilliant, and remarkably mature, second novel."
—*The Economist*

"First-rate. . . . You simply do not realize how anemic most contemporary fiction is until you read Adiga's muscular prose. His plots don't unwind, they surge." —*USA Today*

"With wit and observation, Adiga gives readers a well-rounded portrait of Mumbai in all of its teeming, bleating, inefficient glory. . . . Like any good novelist, Adiga's story lingers because it nestles in the heart and the head."
—*The Christian Science Monitor*

"*Last Man in Tower* is a nuanced study of human nature in all of its complexity and mystery. (It is also humane and funny.) Nothing is quite as it seems in the novel, which makes for surprises both pleasant and disturbing."—*Pittsburgh Post-Gazette*

"Adiga populates his fiction with characters from all parts of India's contemporary social spectrum, and the intensity of his anger . . . impish wit." . . . *Journal*

"Vain, shrewd and stubborn, [Masterji] is one of the most delightfully contradictory characters to appear in recent fiction."
—*The Washington Post*

"Adiga maps out in luminous prose India's ambivalence toward its accelerated growth, while creating an engaging protagonist . . . a man whose ambition and independence have been tempered with an understanding of the important, if almost imperceptible, difference between development and progress."
—*Entertainment Weekly*

"[An] adroit, ruthless and sobering novel. . . . Adiga peppers his universally relevant tour de force with brilliant touches, multiple ironies and an indictment of our nature."   —*The Star Ledger*

"Adiga is an exceptionally talented novelist, and the subtlety with which he presents the battle between India's aspirants and its left-behind poor is exceptional."
—*Richmond Times-Dispatch*

"A brilliant examination of the power of money. . . . Ultimately *Last Man in Tower* is about how greed affects compassion. . . . Adiga skillfully unfolds a surprising conclusion that underscores what a great novel this is."   —*Minneapolis Star-Tribune*

"[Full of] acute observations and sharp imagery. . . . Like all cautionary tales, it embodies more than a little truth about our times."   —*Financial Times*

"Dickensian. . . . Well worth the time of any reader interested in the circumstances of life in a seemingly foreign place that turns out to be awfully familiar. . . . Readers above all else will find pleasure and pain in the ups and downs of the human family itself."   —Alan Cheuse, *San Francisco Chronicle*